Buying
a Property

Australian Edition

by Nicola McDougall
and Bruce Brammall

A Wiley Brand

Buying a Property For Dummies®, Australian Edition

Published by

John Wiley & Sons, Australia Ltd

Level 4, 600 Bourke St, Melbourne, Victoria 3000, Australia

www.dummies.com

Copyright © 2023 John Wiley & Sons Australia, Ltd

The moral rights of the authors have been asserted.

ISBN: 978-1-394-17042-5

A catalogue record for this book is available from the National Library of Australia

All rights reserved. No part of this book, including interior design, cover design and icons, may be reproduced or transmitted in any form, by any means (electronic, photocopying, recording or otherwise) without the prior written permission of the Publisher. Requests to the Publisher for permission should be addressed to the Legal Services section of John Wiley & Sons Australia, Ltd, Level 1, 155 Cremorne Street, Richmond, Vic 3121, or email auspermissions@wiley.com.

Cover image: © Monkey Business Images/Shutterstock

Typeset by Straive

LIMIT OF LIABILITY/DISCLAIMER OF WARRANTY: WHILE THE PUBLISHER AND AUTHORS HAVE USED THEIR BEST EFFORTS IN PREPARING THIS WORK, THEY MAKE NO REPRESENTATIONS OR WARRANTIES WITH RESPECT TO THE ACCURACY OR COMPLETENESS OF THE CONTENTS OF THIS WORK AND SPECIFICALLY DISCLAIM ALL WARRANTIES, INCLUDING WITHOUT LIMITATION ANY IMPLIED WARRANTIES OF MERCHANTABILITY OR FITNESS FOR A PARTICULAR PURPOSE. NO WARRANTY MAY BE CREATED OR EXTENDED BY SALES REPRESENTATIVES, WRITTEN SALES MATERIALS OR PROMOTIONAL STATEMENTS FOR THIS WORK. THE FACT THAT AN ORGANIZATION, WEBSITE, OR PRODUCT IS REFERRED TO IN THIS WORK AS A CITATION AND/ OR POTENTIAL SOURCE OF FURTHER INFORMATION DOES NOT MEAN THAT THE PUBLISHER AND AUTHORS ENDORSE THE INFORMATION OR SERVICES THE ORGANIZATION, WEBSITE, OR PRODUCT MAY PROVIDE OR RECOMMENDATIONS IT MAY MAKE. THIS WORK IS SOLD WITH THE UNDERSTANDING THAT THE PUBLISHER IS NOT ENGAGED IN RENDERING PROFESSIONAL SERVICES. THE ADVICE AND STRATEGIES CONTAINED HEREIN MAY NOT BE SUITABLE FOR YOUR SITUATION. YOU SHOULD CONSULT WITH A SPECIALIST WHERE APPROPRIATE. FURTHER, READERS SHOULD BE AWARE THAT WEBSITES LISTED IN THIS WORK MAY HAVE CHANGED OR DISAPPEARED BETWEEN WHEN THIS WORK WAS WRITTEN AND WHEN IT IS READ. NEITHER THE PUBLISHER NOR AUTHORS SHALL BE LIABLE FOR ANY LOSS OF PROFIT OR ANY OTHER COMMERCIAL DAMAGES, INCLUDING BUT NOT LIMITED TO SPECIAL, INCIDENTAL, CONSEQUENTIAL, OR OTHER DAMAGES.

Trademarks: Wiley, the Wiley logo, For Dummies, the Dummies Man logo, A Reference for the Rest of Us!, The Dummies Way, Making Everything Easier, dummies.com and related trade dress are trademarks or registered trademarks of John Wiley & Sons, Inc. and/or its affiliates in the United States and other countries, and may not be used without written permission. All other trademarks are the property of their respective owners. John Wiley & Sons Australia, Ltd is not associated with any product or vendor mentioned in this book.

Contents at a Glance

Table of Contents

Introduction

Welcome to *Buying a Property For Dummies* — the beginner's guide to buying property.

With each passing year, prospective homeowners and investors seem to become more and more concerned that they will never purchase a home of their own, let alone an investment property. But here's the thing: If we have learned anything in all the years that we've been writing about, analysing, reporting and (in Bruce's case) advising on property markets, it's that the dream of home ownership becomes a reality for most, with many of us going on to own one, two or even three investment properties.

Of course, we do this because we believe in property ownership as a low-risk way to secure our financial futures — plus, the idea of merely surviving on the pension when we retire, perhaps for many decades, is just not palatable for most of us.

Even when property prices seem to have reached unaffordable levels, first-time buyers and investors can always find ways and means to secure their very own slice (or slices) of real estate. These days, they do this in a variety of ways, but the end result is the same — one day their perseverance pays off and they are handed a set of keys to a property that has their name on the title.

Let's be honest, buying your first property, whether it be as a home or an investment, has always been hard, because it takes dedication, commitment and persistence to make it happen — saving for that first deposit, in particular, takes sacrifice. It was the same when people bought their first property back in the 1960s, the same when we bought our first dwellings in the 1990s and 2000s, and it's likely to continue this way for decades to come.

However, books such as this one can help you achieve your dream of property ownership by not only outlining all of the factors that you need to know to ensure you understand what's involved, but also educating you on the 'how, what and where' to buy to ensure that your first property won't be your last.

About This Book

Buying a Property For Dummies covers tried and proven real estate buying and investing strategies that real people, just like you, use to build wealth and achieve their dreams of home ownership.

Unlike with so many property book authors, though, we don't have an alternative agenda in writing this book. Some real estate investing books are little more than promotional materials for high-priced seminars or developments the author is selling. The objective of this book is to give you the best information as a prospective homeowner or property investor, so that, when you buy a property or properties, you can do so wisely and confidently.

Foolish Assumptions

Whenever authors sit down to write books, they have particular audiences in mind. Because of this, they must make some assumptions about who the reader is and what that reader is looking for. Here are a few assumptions that we've made about you:

» You're looking for a way to buy or invest in real estate but don't know what types of properties and strategies are best. (We'll show you.)

» You're considering buying your next home or an investment property — be it a house, a unit, an apartment or flat, or a townhouse in a metro or regional area, but your real estate experience is largely limited to owning your own home or renting.

» You're concerned that the opportunity to buy a home or investment property is passing you by after missing out a few times already or getting caught up in analysis paralysis.

» You might own your home and perhaps one investment property, but don't want to make a mistake when buying your next one because it's too important to your future financial plans and dreams.

» You're just plain frustrated that you haven't yet achieved your dream of property ownership and are looking for some expert assistance to help turn your dream into a real estate reality.

If any of these descriptions hits home for you, you've come to the right place.

Icons Used in This Book

Throughout this book, you can find friendly and useful icons to enhance your reading pleasure and to note specific types of information. Here's what each icon means:

REMEMBER

This icon flags concepts and facts that we want to ensure you remember as you make your real estate purchases and investments.

TECHNICAL STUFF

Included with this icon are complex examples and interesting technical stuff that you may want to read to become even more familiar with the topic.

TIP

This icon points out something that can save you time, headaches, money or all of the above!

WARNING

Here we're trying to direct you away from blunders and errors that others have made when investing in property. This alerts you to those who may have conflicts of interest or offer biased advice, as well as other concerns that could really cost you big bucks.

Where to Go from Here

Buying a Property For Dummies is designed to provide prospective homebuyers and early-stage investors with the education you need to make informed property-buying decisions. Consider this book as the one that will give you a sound overview of many of the key concepts of purchasing real estate as a homebuyer or an investor.

Of course, if you're ready to take the next step or are seeking more advanced and thorough information, you should pick up a copy of *Property Investing For Dummies*, 3rd Australian edition (also written by us and published by Wiley) to help you on your path to successful real estate investment and a prosperous financial future.

Chapter **1**

Getting Ready to Buy Real Estate

B uying a first home or investment property can be a stressful time for many people. Chances are the purchase is going to be the most money you have ever spent on anything in your entire life! But worry not, because you are taking positive action and educating yourself beforehand via this book. The key to successful property selection — either for your home or as an investment property — is recognising that a one-size-fits-all approach is not possible. So, by learning about the different types of residential properties available, as well as some solid investing principles, you're setting yourself up to make savvy purchasing decisions with the potential for sound capital growth in the years ahead.

In this chapter, we take you through some of the basics about buying residential properties, and using your home as a base for buying your first investment property. We also outline some of the benefits of rentvesting — or buying an investment property while continuing to rent in your preferred location.

Purchasing Residential Properties

Residential property can be an attractive real estate investment for many people. Residential housing is easier to understand, purchase and manage than most other types of property, such as office, industrial and retail property. Either as a homeowner or a renter, you already have some level of experience locating the type of property you want to live in, working out how much you can afford, and maintaining that property.

If you've been in the market for a home yourself, you know that, in addition to freestanding (detached) houses, you can choose from numerous types of attached or multi-dwelling properties, including units, apartments and townhouses. In the following sections, we provide an overview of why some of these may make an attractive option for you.

Freestanding houses

From a long-term investment point of view, *freestanding* houses have usually performed better in the long run than attached housing, units or apartments. In a sound real estate market, most housing appreciates, but traditional detached homes tend to out-perform other housing types for the following reasons:

>> Freestanding houses tend to attract more potential buyers — most people, when they can afford it, prefer detached dwellings, particularly for the increased privacy (and space).

>> Attached housing, or units and townhouses, is less expensive and easier to build — and to overbuild. Because of this potential for surplus properties on the market, such property tends to appreciate more moderately in price.

>> Land value is the major driver of property prices — so the higher the land content, the more likely the capital growth. And a freestanding house, in most cases, has a higher proportion of land content than attached housing.

Because freestanding houses are the first choice for most Australians, market prices for such dwellings can sometimes become inflated beyond what's justified by the rental income that they can produce. And even if you're buying the property to live in yourself, potential rental income compared to purchase price is a good indication of whether the property is overprice.

Detached houses are likely to produce lower rental yields (rent as a proportion of current value, for the purpose of market comparison) than most other options, partly because of the higher purchase prices of houses versus units.

As the homeowner, you are responsible for maintenance and repairs of the property. If you're purchasing the property as an investment and you engage a property manager (as we always recommend), your manager will find the tradespeople and coordinate and oversee the work, while the fees for such work will come out of your returns. (See Chapter 3 for more on gathering your expert team.) Also recognise that, if you purchase a house with many fine features and amenities, tenants living in your property won't necessarily treat it with the same tender loving care that you might.

TIP

A primary rule of being a successful landlord is to let go of any emotional attachment to a property. But that sort of attachment on the tenant's part is favourable: The more tenants make your rental property their 'home', the more likely they are to return it to you in good condition — except for the expected normal wear and tear of day-to-day living.

Attached housing

As the cost of land around major cities has skyrocketed, packing more multi-dwelling units into a given plot of land keeps housing somewhat more affordable. Here, we discuss the investment merits of units, apartments, and townhouses — for owner-occupiers and investors alike.

Apartments and units

When you purchase a flat or apartment, you're actually purchasing the airspace and interior surfaces of a specific apartment as well as a proportionate interest in the common areas — the pool, tennis court, grounds, hallways, roof-top gardens and so on. Although you (or your tenants if you're an investor) have full use and enjoyment of the common areas, the body corporate or owners corporation (the collective owners of all apartments in the block) actually owns and maintains the common areas, as well as the building structures themselves, which typically include the foundations, outside walls and doors, roof, and the plumbing, electrical and other building systems. Before purchasing an apartment, you should review the body corporate governing documents to check what's considered common areas, and take into account annual body corporate fees.

A unit, on the other hand, can be an attached or detached dwelling on a block of land, with shared common ground (such as driveways and gardens). Examples include two, three or more dwellings that have been built on a single block of land.

One advantage that apartments and units have over other property options is that most bodies corporate deal with issues such as roofing and gardening for the entire building and receive bulk-buying benefits. *Note:* You're still responsible for maintenance that's needed inside your unit, such as servicing appliances and interior painting. For investors, apartments tend to produce higher yields because of the lower purchase price points.

Although apartments may be somewhat easier to maintain, they tend to appreciate slower than houses and even units, unless they're located in a desirable urban area. This is in part because most apartment blocks lack the scarcity value of houses.

Townhouses

Essentially attached homes, townhouses are a hybrid between 'air space only' apartments and houses. Like apartments and units, townhouses are usually attached, typically sharing walls and a continuous roof. But townhouses are often two- or even three-storey buildings that can come with a courtyard or balcony and offer more privacy than an apartment. That generally means you don't have someone living above or below you.

REMEMBER

As with apartments, it's extremely important that you review the body corporate governing documents before you purchase a townhouse to see exactly what you legally own. Townhouses are usually organised so that no limitations are stipulated on the transferability of ownership of the individual lot that encompasses each dwelling and often a small area of immediately adjacent land or air space for a patio or balcony. Courtyards are often exclusive-use common property, because, although the owner has sole use of the area, the body corporate still owns it. The common areas are all part of a larger single lot, and each owner is a shareholder, in equal proportion, of the common area.

Deciding among the options

Choosing a home to live in yourself is a very personal decision, determined by many factors — including your own lifestyle requirements and the kinds of design elements you find aesthetically pleasing. From a pure investment perspective, my top recommendations for first-time investors are houses or well-located units that offer scarcity value (such as Art Deco design elements) or those with desirable attributes (such as water views).

Apartments make more sense for homebuyers and investors who don't want to deal with building maintenance and security issues. (See Chapter 6 for more on the ongoing costs of real estate.) Avoid shared-wall dwellings (particularly apartments) in inner-city areas where the availability of prime development sites (property allotments ripe for development) makes building many more apartment towers more likely. Apartment prices tend to perform best where nearby land has already been fully (or nearly fully) developed.

TIP

For higher returns as an investor, look for property where relatively simple cosmetic changes can allow you to raise rents, and so increase the market value of the property. Examples of such improvements may include, but aren't limited to:

>> Adding fresh paint and floor coverings

>> Improving the landscaping

>> Upgrading the kitchen with new appliances and new cabinet and drawer hardware

All the preceding changes can totally change the look and feel of the property.

TIP

Whether you're buying for yourself or as an investor, look for property with a great location and good physical condition but with some maintenance that the current owner has put off — for example, a property with a large yard but dead grass, or a two- or three-car garage but with peeling paint or a broken garage door. These cosmetic issues can help keep the purchase price down. Then you can develop a hit list of items to achieve maximum results for minimum dollars. As well as fixing the paintwork, for example, you could also add a remote garage door opener to jazz up the property for minimum cost. You might be surprised how much aesthetic appeal and value you can add to a property owned by a burnt-out, absentee, or totally uninterested owner who's tired of maintaining the property.

REMEMBER

Unless you can afford a large deposit (20 to 30 per cent or more), the early years of property ownership may financially challenge you, depending on the type of property:

>> **Houses:** The early years of owning a property are usually the most difficult financially, particularly with houses. The reason: Land value. Houses sell at a premium, especially relative to the rent they command because the land itself has a lower rental value than the dwelling.

>> **Apartments or apartment buildings:** Apartments and apartment buildings, particularly those with many dwellings, are generally more affordable to purchase and, for investors, occasionally can produce a small positive cash flow, even in the early years of ownership.

See Chapter 2 for more on buying strategies once you have narrowed down your property options, and see Chapters 4 and 5 for more on financing your purchase and mortgages.

Using Your Home as a Base for Investing

The first foray into property purchasing for most people is a home in which to live. In the following sections, we not only cover the advantages inherent in buying a home for your own use, but also explain why a home and an investment property are essentially mutually exclusive purchases (except in the case of holiday homes). We also cover the implications of converting your home to a rental property, as well as fixing it up and selling it.

REMEMBER

An important concept to understand is that a 'home' is not an 'investment property' from the perspective of investing. The two types of assets have too many differences, particularly when it comes to tax treatment, for them to be talked about as the same thing. However, it is important to always consider every home you buy as an investment because of the significant financial outlay that is required. In this book, when you see the word 'home', we're talking about the dwelling in which you live (also known in tax terms as the *principal place of residence*). However, 'investment property' can pretty much cover any other property on which an income, usually rent, is earned.

REMEMBER

Although a home is not an investment property technically, for most people their home is the basis from which most investment property is bought. The equity that has built up, for people who have owned their own home for a few years and have seen the value of their home grow and their loan reduce, becomes the cornerstone from which real wealth is built. The equity can be used as security for other investments in property. Outside of a large cash deposit, banks see home equity as the best source of security for their customers to use to reinvest.

Why tax makes 'home' and 'investment' different

What separates the taxation treatment of homes from that of rented properties is the federal government's intention that the principal place of residence (home) should not be taxed, whereas investment properties should be taxed on the profits or income made in the same way that all other economic investments are taxed.

The first major difference is capital gains tax (CGT) — a home is generally exempt from CGT when sold. How much money you've made on your home doesn't matter. If the property has truly always simply been your home, you do not pay CGT on any profit you make. If you initially paid $500,000 for your home, for example, and you sell it for $2 million, you won't have to pay CGT — not a cent. Making the same profit on an investment property is a different story. You do have to pay CGT. (For more information on CGT and how it's charged, you can check out our larger title *Property Investing For Dummies*, 3rd Australian Edition, published by Wiley. You can also go to the website for the Australian Tax Office — www.ato.gov.au.)

The second major tax difference between your home and an investment property is in the treatment of expenses incurred in relation to a property. By *expenses*, we mean the ongoing costs of holding or maintaining a property, such as mortgage interest, construction or capital-improvement costs, maintenance costs and government imposts. Usually, these expenses aren't tax-deductible for homeowners, but are deductible for an investment property. Tax deductibility makes a big difference to the real cost of an item. Homeowners who pay $200 to change the locks on their front door get no deduction. But an investor who pays $200 for the same work can have a proportion of the cost returned through tax (depending on the investor's marginal tax rate), which effectively reduces the cost of the same work.

Buying a place of your own

During your adult life, you're going to need a roof over your head for many decades. You have two options: Either buy a place to live in yourself or pay someone else rent to live in a property they own. Real estate is the only purchase or investment that you can either live in or rent out to produce income. Shares, bonds or managed funds can't provide a roof over your head — or anyone else's either!

REMEMBER

Unless you expect to move within the next few years, buying a property to call home probably makes good long-term financial sense. (Even if you relocate, you may decide to continue owning the property and rent it out.) Owning usually costs less than renting over the long haul (your loan gets locked in at the start and becomes progressively smaller in real terms as the years roll on, while rents continue to rise) and allows you to build *equity* in an asset (the difference between market value and loans against the property).

You can briefly consider your home as part of your investment portfolio when you use that home as the cornerstone of your wealth-creation plans. It's usually the biggest single investment that you make. It's also usually responsible for creating equity that you can later use to make further investments (such as buying investment properties). Many people move to a less costly home when they retire (known as *downsizing*). Downsizing in retirement frees up the equity you've built up over years of home ownership. You can use this money to supplement your retirement income and superannuation, and for any other purpose your heart desires.

Another way your home is similar to an investment is that your home usually appreciates in value over the years, and you can use that money to further your financial or personal goals. You can also turn your home into an investment property if you decide to buy and move into another property. But at this point — particularly for tax purposes — the former home stops being a 'home' and becomes an 'investment property', and your new home gets the tax advantages and disadvantages of becoming your home.

Converting your home to a rental

Turning your current home into a rental property when you move or upgrade is one way to buy and own more properties. Holding on to your current home when you're buying a new one can be advisable if you're moving into a larger home or moving inter-state. This approach presents a number of positives:

>> You save the time and cost of finding a separate rental property, not to mention the associated transaction costs.

>> You know the property and have probably taken good care of it and perhaps made some improvements.

>> You know the target market because the house appealed to you at an earlier stage of life.

WARNING

Many people hold on to their current home for the wrong reasons when they buy another. This often happens in a depressed market — even though they're buying a new home at a lower price, at the same time they're facing the prospect of selling their former home for a reduced price. If you plan to move and want to keep your current home as a long-term investment property, you can. But turning your home into a *short-term* rental is usually a bad move because:

>> You may not want the responsibilities of being a landlord, yet you force yourself into the landlord business if you convert your home into a rental.

>> You may have to pay some capital gains tax (CGT) — proportionate to the time you owned the property as an investment versus a home — on any profit when you do sell it.

TIP

If you own a property as a home but don't live in it — because you've moved interstate, for example, and are renting while you live there — you may be able to hang on to it for as long as six years before you incur CGT, even if you put a tenant into the property. This law applies only if you don't claim another 'home' as a principal place of residence in the meantime.

TIP

If you do convert your home into an investment property, you may be able to claim tax deductions for portions of the capital improvements that you made to the property while it was your home, depending on the relevant legislation at the time.

Considering Rentvesting

An increasingly popular investment strategy over the past decade is what's known as *rentvesting*. In essence, this strategy involves investors, usually first-time ones but not always, buying a property elsewhere while continuing to rent in their location of choice. High property prices in cities such as Sydney and Melbourne are no doubt one of the reasons this investment strategy has become so popular, because it enables people to invest their funds without sacrificing their current lifestyle. For example, they may only be able to afford to buy property in an outer-fringe city suburb or even a regional area. They can make this investment, and get started in the property market, while continuing to rent in their current location.

Rentvesting is becoming such a common investment strategy that, according to the 2022 Property Investment Professionals of Australia (PIPA) Annual Investor Sentiment Survey, 29 per cent of first-time investors are using it, with 45 per cent of all investors indicating they would consider rentvesting personally as well.

Generally speaking, young people can often afford to rent in locations where they would not be able to afford to purchase a property, so rentvesting gives them the best of both worlds so to speak — they are investing when they are younger while still enjoying all of the attributes of living in their suburb of choice.

Chapter **2**

Understanding Buying Strategies

The multimillion-dollar question has always been how do you know how, where, what, and when to buy real estate?! We have always believed the best time to purchase is when it's the right time for you personally — regardless of what the market is doing at the time. That's because you should always consider property ownership as a long-term decision, which means that any market wrinkles will be ironed out over your many years of ownership.

In this chapter, we take a brief look at some of the most common methods of purchasing property — whether as a home or an investment — and we tell you what we think about whether you should pursue these options. We start off with a discussion on how to purchase via private sales, auctions and tenders. We then cover getting a jump on the market through off-market sales.

Buying Property Strategies

Opportunities to purchase real estate are near boundless. Every city, town or suburb has people trying to sell for one reason or another. The task for the property buyer is to sort the wheat from the chaff — finding the best properties from the pool of those available on the market. This is where real estate sales agents come in — they're a central place for buyers and sellers to channel their separate interests.

When you find a property, however, how does it change hands between owners? Obviously, through a sale. Properties are sold in three main ways — private treaty sale, public auction and tender.

Private treaty sales

Across Australia, the most common way for properties to change hands is through private treaty sale, or simply private sale. When the owner of a property decides she wants to sell by private sale, she places the asking price she wants on the property listing and then waits for offers to come in, usually via the real estate sales agent she has appointed.

In most stages of the property cycle, both vendor and potential purchaser then negotiate. The seller wants $800,000. A buyer comes in with an offer of $785,000. The seller lowers her price to $795,000. The buyer raises her offer to $790,000. And the haggling and changing of position keep going until the property is sold. Or not sold. Properties put up for private sale can be sold very quickly — often before they've even really been advertised. But they can also take months (even a year or more) to sell in a particularly slow market or when the seller has unrealistic expectations of what the property is worth.

The private sale market is all about negotiation. Potential buyers usually have plenty of properties on the market to choose from. And there's usually no rush (when compared with auction, with the process of purchasing literally over within 30 minutes). Negotiations can last for days, sometimes weeks.

TIP

A non-negotiable sale is rare when it comes to private selling. For a start, most property sellers start with a price a little above what they really see as their lower limit. If they're really determined to get a minimum of $800,000 for the property, for example, they may start their sales campaign with a price of $825,000 in the hope they'll be able to negotiate a price somewhere between $799,000 and $810,000.

Prices are almost always negotiable. And it's sometimes up to buyers to be persuasive about what they believe the market value of the property is. You can try to get a seller to reduce her expectations through a number of means (although you'll usually be dealing with the seller's agent, who'll be wise to most of these tricks). Often, it's as simple as getting a builder, building inspector or valuer to point out the property's flaws, showing how much fixing these problems is going to cost.

Buyers' agents can be a very useful part of your team too, particularly during negotiations. Putting your professional buyers' agent up against a real estate sales agent can be like throwing suited lawyers into a locked room together. But buyers' agents know sales agents' tricks and vice versa. Experienced buyers' agents take the emotion out — you're likely to be emotional, especially if buying a property to be your home, but they're not. And removing emotion is always important in property negotiations where you're talking about large sums of money. (See Chapter 3 for more on finding a buyers' agent.)

REMEMBER

Experienced real estate sales agents can be a curse to deal with, or they can be your best helper. A sales agent's primary and fiduciary responsibility is to their vendors (their clients), and they'll obviously be more loyal to their clients than to prospective buyers. But agents also often believe that their clients' expectations are unrealistic and will use all offers, sometimes even a very low one, as a way of conditioning clients that the price they expect for their property is too high.

TIP

In most states and territories of Australia, purchases made through private sale treaties come with a cooling-off period, where buyers can change their mind and get out of the sale contract. The period starts at midnight on the day the contract is signed and lasts for up to five business days. A decision to exercise your right to a cooling-off period may incur penalties (usually quite small). Sellers don't have the right to a cooling-off period.

Public auctions

Let's be honest, buying property at auction is a strategy that scares many people. But it really shouldn't, since auctions are the most transparent way to purchase real estate — everyone present sees what the market is prepared to pay for the property. A good auction can be a thrilling spectacle, with the drama played out on suburban streets and footpaths — sometimes bidding is so intense, and the price achieved so out-of-the-box, that it causes uninvolved spectators to audibly gasp and even break into applause when a 'winner' is finally determined.

Auctions are commonplace in Melbourne, Sydney and Brisbane, and they're used by real estate agents in many other parts of the country. The aim of auctions is to create an intense atmosphere for the sales process. Within a period of 10 or 15 minutes (after the particulars of the property have been read out), a property can be sold — unless, of course, it's passed in because it hasn't reached the reserve price the vendor has set (see the sidebar 'Passed in: Post-auction negotiation'). Unless you're the one making the final bid, you're not buying the property, and you have to continue your search.

The auction process is always under scrutiny. Occasionally, mooted moves are proposed to impose restrictions on auctions following media noise citing concerns from buyers who've missed out on properties or believe that agents have misled them over the likely sales price of a property. These concerns appear to be cyclical and seem to get the most airplay when property prices are rising, and people are feeling locked out of the market.

TIP

Regardless of whether you're purchasing the property as a home or an investment, if you're considering bidding at an auction, set yourself firm limits before you attend. If you've spotted the property at the start of its marketing period, you usually have about three or four weeks before the auction to do your due diligence — you can't do that after an auction. No cooling-off period (refer to the preceding section) is offered in public auction sales. Several days before the auction, nail down what you believe is fair value for the property. Then try to bid only up to that price. If your research suggests that a fair price for a unit is $800,000, set your limit at that price with the aim of only picking up the property if it goes for $800,000 or below. If you are purchasing as an investor, this purchase is about making money — it's much harder to achieve your goal if you overpay for the asset in the first place. Stay focused — and don't get emotional.

PASSED IN: POST-AUCTION NEGOTIATION

Auctions often fail to get sufficient interest or momentum from bidders to move bids to a point that's acceptable for the vendor to sell. Auctions can get off to a slow start and not get any faster. After a few lacklustre bids, the auctioneer declares the final bid to be insufficient and that 'the property will now be passed in'. What happens then?

If no genuine bidders turned up, or only one bidder, and no real auction took place, the property usually effectively reverts to a private treaty sale. If the agent can't get an acceptable bid, she'll place the property back on the market with a 'For Sale' sticker that afternoon.

If several bidders showed up, the house will be passed in. The highest bidder will probably be ushered inside (but not always) by an agent and told what the vendor's reserve is (say, $800,000). Other agents (sometimes two or three other agents, including the auctioneer, attend every auction) will try to keep the next highest underbidder (or underbidders) around to let them know they still have a chance. The highest bidder will usually have the first crack at the vendor's reserve. If she isn't prepared to pay the reserve price, then agents will likely offer the property to the other bidders.

Here lies the strangeness of this situation and an interesting insight into the pressure tactics used by agents. They already have the person who's offered the most money for this property inside — in a competitive auction, other interested parties have already fallen by the wayside, believing the price was too high. But agents want to keep the auction going by having one agent negotiating with the highest bidder and another agent working on getting another bid or two out of parties who've already thrown in the towel.

Auctions are all about competition and pressure. If you've seen off your competitors, you're in the box seat. The market has spoken, and you value the property more highly than anyone else. If you value it a little higher (which you inevitably do because auctions rarely get the top bid out of the final bidder), there's no harm in raising your bid a little. But, for an investment property, don't go too high. This is a business decision — don't allow emotions to get the better of you. The fact that you were prepared to pay more is irrelevant, and the risk that vendors take when they decide to auction.

WARNING

Agents' auction practices tend to come under scrutiny when buyers watch prices soar 20 to 30 per cent (or more) above the estimate or comparative recent sales offered during the property's marketing period. The concern over what's known as *underquoting*, whether valid or not, has undermined confidence in the auction process in the past. If a property being auctioned has a reserve price from the vendors of, say, $800,000, agents often advertise the property in a variety of ways to attract potential buyers — including putting their estimated price range below this reserve.

The rule is an unwritten one, but agents tend to estimate their price range within about 10 per cent below the vendor's potential reserve. The vendor can then change their mind at the last moment to raise or lower their reserve. That's out of an agent's power.

A problem during booming market conditions is when bidders push the price well in excess of the estimated range — underbidders feel like they've wasted their time because the budget they have means they were never really in the running to buy the house.

TIP

Don't get too worried about the debate over underquoting (or its opposite, *overquoting*, which is what agents often do to vendors to get their business in the first place). If you do your homework and look thoroughly at prices in the area, you'll have a reasonable idea of whether the property is within your price range. And, in any case, as soon as bidding tops what you believe is fair value, your interest should immediately stop — especially if you're purchasing as an investor. Even if it happens mid-auction, you should walk away from the property (in your mind, if not in body) and start thinking about the next property you're interested in.

Tenders

Many names exist and slightly different processes are used for what's essentially a *sale by tender* — you submit a bid via a number of methods by a set deadline. These bids are also known as *sale by set date*, *set sales* and *expressions of interest*. They all have varying degrees of similarity to tenders, although some might be part-auction, with negotiations opening up with the highest bidder.

AUCTIONS VERSUS PRIVATE SALES

The argument over whether auctions or private treaty sales produce the best returns is unlikely to be settled — it's a perpetual debate. But there seems to be little doubt that, under the right conditions, auctions have the potential to deliver results that seem to defy logic.

How does an auction achieve these results? Simply, two (or more) people attend the same auction with huge budgets at their disposal. They both love this house and have decided that its value to them is substantially higher than the figure put on it by the vendor, the agent or the majority of the rest of the people in the market.

It's not unheard of during a particularly strong property market for a property being advertised for $800,000 to $1 million to go for $1.2 million or $1.4 million. Five bidders may be prepared to pay $1 million, but when it hits that price, all but two bidders fall away and the last two slug it out, a few thousand dollars at a time, until the second-last person withdraws.

This situation is what a vendor dreams about — two bidders desperate to buy the property for one reason or another. Indeed, 'It only takes two' is a common saying in the real estate sector. The bidders may have no idea of the value of property in the area. They may have a vision for the property that others don't share. They may have been the underbidders on so many occasions that they're prepared to pay a premium just so they don't have to continue the search. In most cases, 'silly' prices achieved at auction aren't going to come from investors — unless they're developers who can see an enormous potential for the land. Prices that defy logic usually come from emotional homebuyers.

And what happens to properties that get passed in during an auction? Little reliable data on those properties exists, except that they tend to be sold later through a private treaty sale. A good deal of those properties sell fairly quickly, but at what discount on the price the vendor was hoping for?

Private sales, on the other hand, don't put the same intense pressure on the buyer or the seller. People have time to think about the offer they're going to make, and sellers have time to think about whether or not they will accept it.

The tender process is very rarely used for the sale of residential investment properties, but it's not unknown. Most properties offered through a tender-style process are commercial properties, particularly higher value properties.

Tenders require you to put your own value on the property. Prior to getting to this stage, you make your price estimation of the property by either comparing the prices of other similar properties in that suburb, or by getting a qualified valuer to do the job. Normally you only get one shot, so the price you submit should be at, or very near to, the top price you're prepared to pay

This scenario is the same with multiple offer situations in private treaty sales, with potential buyers generally only having one opportunity to submit their 'highest and best offer' on a property if a number of potential purchasers are competing against each other.

Taking Advantage of Off-Market Sales

The 'Holy Grail' of property buying opportunities is *off-market sales*. These properties are usually offered to a select group of potential buyers, including buyers' agents, before they are marketed publicly.

While these properties are generally still being sold by private treaty, they have not been publicly advertised. A vendor or a sales agent might want to use this sales method for a number of reasons. The vendor might not want the property sale to be in the public forum, usually due to privacy reasons or perhaps a divorce. It could be a marketing ploy in slower market conditions, because those buyers will think they are being offered a special opportunity to buy the property 'off-market' without as much competition.

Off-market properties are much more prevalent in slower market conditions, but they can be available in a boom market, too. Regardless of the market conditions, it is vital that you not only understand the opportunity in front of you, but also ensure you know the market price for the property because you could easily overpay for the 'privilege'.

IN THIS CHAPTER

» Putting a team together

» Starting with a solicitor

» Seeking lending professionals

» Hiring an accountant

» Choosing a building inspector

» Finding buying and selling agents

Chapter **3**

Finding Your Expert Team

The real estate world has evolved significantly over the past few decades, with higher standards of business practice among property professionals. The numbers of experts who can assist homebuyers and investors with their buying hopes and dreams has also sharply increased.

Of course, you need to confirm that the 'expert' you're considering working with is, in fact, an expert and has plenty of experience in the chosen field — whether that be as a buyers' agent, mortgage broker or conveyancer. The very best operators have all of the appropriate licences and are generally members of their industry associations as well.

In this chapter, we discuss the different professionals involved in real estate who you can team up with as you search for property ownership opportunities and proceed with the purchase of real estate.

Establishing Your Team Early

Some real estate buyers make the mistake of looking for a property to purchase without spending any time up-front identifying the professionals whose help should be hired.

TIP

Having your team in place before you begin your serious property searching is necessary for two reasons:

>> **You can move quickly.** The speed at which you can close a transaction is an advantage in any type of market. In a buyers' market, some sellers are desperate for cash and need to exit quickly. In a sellers' market, sellers typically won't tolerate a long settlement if another buyer can get them their asking price sooner.

>> **You can effectively research the property before making an offer.** Prudent homebuyers and investors conduct their research before they make an offer. You don't want to waste time on a property that can't meet your goals or your budget.

TIP

For individual residential properties, if you do find yourself in a position where you have to move quickly, consider making a *conditional offer* for a property — one that's subject to finance, for example, which should be standard for all purchases anyway, apart from those bought at auction. In many senses, doing extensive research on the property — getting building and pest inspections — is pointless if the seller's asking price isn't in your ballpark. Making a conditional offer can help determine whether the seller's asking price has any leeway. We recommend making offers only when you've done enough investigating to feel comfortable that your further thorough review of the property interiors (and rental track record for investors) probably won't reveal any surprises that will lead to cancelling the purchase. (See Chapter 8 for more on formal due diligence once a conditional offer has been accepted.)

WARNING

Never make unconditional offers to buy property without having first consulted your key professionals — your banker, mortgage broker or lender, and your solicitor. Avoid making an offer if you don't have the cash or finance ready; also avoid making offers if you haven't had a solicitor (or conveyancer) cast their eyes over the legal documents. You may invest dozens of hours and several thousand dollars to perform the necessary due diligence (meaning your research), but this amount is small compared with the potential loss from the purchase of a property with problems.

Getting Good Legal Advice

Don't think for a second that you can get away with buying property without getting proper legal advice. This is simply dangerous. Given that vendors sell their property by *caveat emptor* (Latin for 'let the buyer beware'), buyers have an underlying responsibility to know what they're buying. That's understandable. Why would sellers point out reasons for you not to buy their property?

The legal transfer of property from one owner to another is called *conveyancing* — and it's not as simple as signing a few documents. Conveyancing is also about making sure the right taxes and duties are paid, that the correct titles are changing hands and the required legal checks are undertaken.

Choosing your solicitor

You may think that adding a lawyer to your real estate purchasing team is a luxury you can't afford. Well, property conveyancing isn't all that expensive (usually between $1,000 and $2,000) and, unless you're fluent in property law, that's a cheap price to pay to have someone look after it for you.

TIP

We strongly suggest you consult with an experienced real estate solicitor from day one of your life as a property investor. If you've already engaged a solicitor, as soon as you find a property that you're considering making a bid for, you can send your solicitor the sale documents to look over for any interesting or unusual conditions, caveats and easements.

With more complicated transactions, have the solicitor review all documents. A good property solicitor can help ensure you avoid some pitfalls before even making an offer.

REMEMBER

If you're an investor and going beyond single-home dwellings, seek a solicitor who has experience in purchasing and lease transactions. Ideally, you'll find one solicitor or law firm that can assist you with not only your transactions, but also the drafting and review of other documents. In particular, look for solicitors who have specialised knowledge of tenancy laws and the complicated issues surrounding commercial leases.

Regardless of whether you're a homebuyer or investor, find a solicitor with the communication skills to explain legal terms simply to you. As with any professional, the old adage that 'you get what you pay for' holds true more often than not. So, remember that paying a lower hourly rate for a solicitor isn't necessarily your best option.

Solicitors versus conveyancers

Property buyers can use either solicitors or conveyancers, but which is best? The difference in cost between the two is minimal — you can expect to pay somewhere between $1,000 and $2,000 for either, which may not include inescapable fees for some government searches and additional searches.

Solicitors claim that, as a profession, they offer buyers better legal protection if something goes wrong. Conveyancers argue that, if any extra legal protection is involved, it's actually to protect the lawyers themselves from their clients.

REMEMBER

Choosing between a solicitor and a conveyancer is up to you, and often depends on what your legal needs are. For example, simple real estate transactions generally only require the services of conveyancers, but more complex deals, such as purchasing a unit block or a property with development potential, may need the expertise of a solicitor.

Lining Up a Lender or Mortgage Broker

Before looking at specific property opportunities, you need a budget. And, because your budget for real estate purchases is directly a function of how much you can borrow, you need to determine the limits on your borrowing power. If you can't afford a property, how great the deal is doesn't matter at all.

Reviewing roles

Postpone that appointment to look at potential properties until after you've examined the loans available. You have two resources to consult:

>> *Lender* **is a generic term for any firm, or officer of that firm, that lends you the cash to purchase your property.** Most often, your list of possible lenders includes banks, credit unions, building societies, non-bank lenders and private lenders, including property sellers.

>> **A** *mortgage broker* **is a service provider who presents your request for a loan to a variety of different lenders in order to find the best financing for your particular needs.** Just like insurance brokers, a good mortgage broker can be a real asset to your team.

Lenders and mortgage brokers are in the business of making loans. That's how they make money. A lender's product is cash, and they make money by renting that cash to people and businesses that pay them the money back plus interest, which is the cost of renting the money. Money is a commodity just like anything else and its availability and pricing are subject to an assortment of variables.

WARNING

Lenders and mortgage brokers want to find you money for your next real estate purchase, but they're not necessarily objective advisers to provide counsel for how much you should borrow. They're trained to calculate the maximum that you may borrow. Don't confuse this figure with the amount that you can truly afford or that will fit best with your overall financial and personal situation.

REMEMBER

If lenders and mortgage brokers want to find you money, then why is getting a loan so difficult sometimes? Because lenders want to make loans to those homebuyer and investors who are a good credit risk, with a high probability of meeting the repayments. Lenders have costs of doing business and need to make a profit. Because the money they lend often belongs to their depositors, lenders need to be careful and selective about the loans they make.

The lender requires collateral for protection against the borrower not being able to make the debt service payments as required. Collateral is the real or personal property that's pledged to secure a loan or mortgage. If the debt isn't paid as agreed, the lender has the right to force the sale of the collateral to recover the outstanding principal and interest on the loan. Typically, the property being purchased is the pledged collateral for real estate loans or mortgages.

Building relationships

A good lender or mortgage broker can help you understand how your financial situation is likely to affect how much you're able to borrow, before you begin your search for a property.

TIP

Get together with your lender or mortgage broker and provide him with your latest financials, which includes your income and expenses, as well as your assets and liabilities. Always be truthful. One way to sabotage a relationship with a lender or mortgage broker is to exaggerate or stretch the truth about your financial situation or the potential of your proposed property acquisition.

The lender will require supporting documents for your income and assets and will obtain a credit report. Banks weren't born yesterday — they still issue their share of loans that turn sour, but they don't issue a lot of them because they have thorough systems in place. Expect the lender to check and recheck every line item. When you don't oversell yourself or your proposed property, lenders are often more willing to work with you and even offer better terms.

Lenders can also serve a valuable role in preventing you from making serious mistakes. Particularly in overheated markets, where prices are rising irrationally with no fundamental economic support, lenders, through their lending process, can keep you from getting caught up in a buy-at-any-price frenzy, similar to what occurred in some locations before the global financial crisis (GFC) in 2007 and during the COVID-19 pandemic boom in 2021.

In these rapidly rising markets, lenders tend to be more conservative and will limit loan amounts and require larger deposits, as they did in Australia in 2008 and 2022 when global credit issues emerged. These factors provide the lender with additional protection should market prices fall, but they're also a signal that the lender feels the requested loan exceeds the intrinsic value of the property that the lender will be stuck with if you default.

REMEMBER

Small loan offers with high deposits are a clue that you may be paying more than a property is worth or buying at the market's peak.

Adding an Accountant

An accountant may not be the first person you think to consult when making a real estate transaction. However, a good accountant who is a specialist in property investment can provide terrific feedback on the benefits and pitfalls of different strategies. Accountants aren't legally allowed to provide investment advice in Australia (without having additional qualifications). But their knowledge of tax issues can be useful. Of course, make sure your tax professional has experience with property purchasing and investment, preferably with specialist qualifications, and understands your needs and goals.

TIP

Although you may pick up a lot of information about buying real estate and discover some of the advantages of property investing by speaking with some tax people, don't rely on generic information ('Investing in real estate offers a terrific tax dodge', for example). You need specific feedback and ideas from a specialist accountant regarding your unique financial situation and which types of real estate purchases and investments will work best for you.

Based on your age, income and other important factors, the benefits you seek from real estate may be entirely different from what other buyers are after. Many investors, for example, look for immediate cash flow from their properties. But others have sufficient other income currently and prefer to look at real estate as a wealth builder via capital growth to improve their retirement. These investors may be prepared to consider negative gearing as a way of accelerating the potential growth. Those buying the property to live in will have different priorities again.

REMEMBER

While some real estate investors are looking for tax benefits, the ability to negatively gear property should never be the sole reason for investing in property.

The role of your accountant is to evaluate the potential tax ramifications of your purchase or investment and how these aspects will affect your financial position. Remember the old adage, 'It's not what you make that matters, but what you keep'.

A good accountant with property experience can advise you on the proper structures to consider from a tax perspective, as a home-buyer or as an investor. If you are purchasing as an investor, your accountant can advise you on what your best real estate investment might be — the direct ownership of residential investment properties, perhaps, or units in a commercial property trust with lower returns but fewer management headaches, for example. Accountants are tax experts and the ownership structure you choose for your real estate investments can be an important determinant of your success as a property investor.

Meet with your accountant and get to know the benefits and pitfalls of your proposed real estate purchases before you start making offers, even if only so your accountant can suggest which ownership option is best for you.

Inspecting with a Building Expert

Whether or not the building you're buying is brand new, you should never buy a property before you've had a well-qualified builder conduct a thorough inspection of the property. New properties can have serious problems if the builder was shonky or cut corners. And older properties inevitably have maintenance issues.

The two reports you should purchase prior to buying a property are a building report and a pest-inspection report — each of which cost about $400 to $600, depending on a few factors, including size and location of the dwelling. Only commission these reports when some of the other pegs on the property have fallen into place. Building and pest inspections are like getting a full medical for the building — they give you a great insight into current problems and what problems are lurking that are likely to require action within a few years

TIP

The timing of building and pest inspections is important. If you're buying privately, you should make your purchase offer conditional on satisfactory building and pest-inspection reports, which can give you an out for your offer if the reports show major flaws or costly problems. However, you can't do this if you're buying at an auction, where bidding is final. These reports can take a few days to put together, so book in your inspections about a week prior to auction.

The building industry professionals who do your building and pest inspections are able to report on the quality or condition of a range of items, including the structural integrity of the building, plumbing and drainage, insulation, evidence of asbestos, rising damp or termite infestation, roofing quality, sub-floor ventilation, condition of walls and paintwork, and whether additions have had proper council approval.

In the worst-case scenario, they may find serious problems that will cost big money to fix. The cost of fixing these problems may be prohibitive and your interest in the property may end. In most cases, the amount of serious work that needs to be done is quite small.

TIP

The builder's report can sometimes be used to renegotiate the price with a vendor. If costly problems that require fixing arise, pointing them out could see the vendor, particularly one who's had the property on the market for longer than average, reduce his price expectations.

Inspection reports are important because they're one way of being able to control the risks associated with your property purchase. They allow you to plan ahead for those expenses.

One of the largest national groups that provide inspections is the architect's association Archicentre (www.archicentre.com.au). Another way to find a company that provides building inspections in your area is to search online and check out the reviews posted for each company. You can also ask your expert team members for their recommendations.

Working with Real Estate Professionals to Buy and Sell Property

The real estate industry is a considerable sector in Australia, and real estate agents are responsible for the buying and selling of property, and for managing rentals. Although the primary job of agents is to market and sell property, a second, smaller industry group, known as *buyers' agents*, can source and secure property for you.

We cover working with these professionals in the following sections.

Understanding what agents do

Buying property in Australia almost always involves dealing with a licensed real estate agent (although some people do sell their own properties — or attempt to, as it usually turns out). Agents are hired by vendors to sell their property with the aim of getting the highest price possible. In a nutshell, the agent's responsibility is to look after advertising and marketing the property, showing potential buyers through the property, answering queries and then, if it gets to the negotiation stage, acting as the intermediary between buyer and seller.

In most instances, agents charge a commission based on the price a property sells for. This fee is paid by the seller and generally ranges between 1 and 4 per cent, depending on location, value of the property, reputation of the agent and competition in the area.

Obviously, in order to get a sale, the buyer and seller must agree on a price. If a buyer is offering to pay only $760,000 for a property and the seller wants $790,000, no sale occurs. The agent's responsibility in this common situation is to get the buyer and the seller to come together. This usually involves the agent trying to convince the buyer to raise his price and also convincing the vendor to lower his price expectations — known as *conditioning* a vendor.

TIP

No matter what you think of real estate sales agents, it doesn't pay to put them offside if you're looking around a particular area and you're likely to bump into them frequently at house inspections. Be friendly to them and make polite conversation. But, as a potential buyer, don't get sucked in by questions designed to find out how big your budget is. Nothing is better for an agent than knowing how much a potential buyer is looking to spend or could spend if the right property surfaced. If you say that you're looking to spend up to $900,000, the agent now knows that's how much money you can spend. This could hurt you in several ways. An agent has no incentive to show a $700,000 property to a buyer who has $900,000 to spend, even if the property (or investment) may be better. And, if you're bidding at auction, the agent and auctioneer know your limit.

On the lookout: Buyers' agents and QPIAs

Licensed buyers' agents and qualified property investment advisers (QPIAs) are industry professionals who work independently and exclusively for buyers to help them find and secure a home or investment property.

WARNING

The number of buyers' agents and QPIAs has been rising in Australia over the past decade — as has a less qualified cohort. Some people present themselves as being a buyers' advocate, for example, but don't have the skills, experience or qualifications to back up their claims. When considering buyers' agents or QPIAs, make sure you check their qualifications and their bona fides, such as their membership of relevant industry associations, the Property Investment Professionals of Australia (PIPA) and the Real Estate Buyers Agents Association of Australia (REBAA), before agreeing to work with them.

The most professional, educated and experienced buyers' agents and QPIAs will provide you with a tailored purchasing or investment plan that is bespoke to you personally, and will charge you a fee for their professional service, as is their right. They will also happily disclose any commissions that they are paid, and by whom, because they are committed to transparency.

Understanding the advantages of buyers' agents

Buyers' agents are becoming a bigger part of the property buying landscape, especially for time-poor homebuyers and investors. They can add significant value and potentially save you thousands — if not tens of thousands — of dollars by being able to deal impartially with the seller's agent. They can also use their deeper local connections in the area or industry to source the best properties for you specifically.

Many homebuyers and property investors do their own homework and research and are prepared to save themselves the buyers' agent fee to find their own properties, especially if they're looking to invest in single-home dwellings. But experienced buyers' agents can remove many risks for you, which can far outweigh their direct cost, especially for investors seeking properties interstate to take advantage of different market conditions.

Firstly, buyers' agents are often able to spot under market value properties and can potentially negotiate the price of properties down, which may potentially save you far more than the fee you've paid for their professional services. Secondly, they usually have a clear buying or investment strategy you can take advantage of.

TIP

Make sure the buyers' agent you're considering has a solid track record and that you understand what his investment strategy is and how that might be different from your own. Some buyers' agents recommend property that minimises tax (such as property that is negatively geared or new). Others have a different focus — for example, they only purchase properties that are new, are neutrally geared, are a certain distance from a central business district, have certain types of characteristics, or are located in growth hotspots around the nation.

REMEMBER

Each property buying strategy has its benefits and drawbacks, and understanding how these might apply to your situation is crucially important. For example, if you're looking to invest and you don't have a lot of spare income, a negatively geared property may have too big an impact on your personal cash flow. A less aggressive option may suit your circumstances better. Similarly, if cash flow isn't your issue, a neutrally geared property may not be as beneficial to your long-term wealth-creation plans.

A third possible advantage of buyers' agents is that you have a professional dealing with a professional — a buyers' agent dealing with a sales agent. When that's happening, the emotion is completely removed from the discussions between these two professionals, especially in the negotiation phase of the real estate transaction.

Fourthly, your buyers' agent can give you back your time. Choosing property can be a horrendously time-consuming process, from searching through the properties online, to attending inspections, to objectively assessing them (or trying to), to getting the inspections done, to making offers or bidding at auction, to settling the purchase. It can take dozens and dozens (even hundreds) of hours to find property that suits your needs. Depending on how you value your time — and you should put a dollar value on your time — the cost of a buying professional could be justified simply on the time they save you (outside of the other benefits already covered in this section).

Considering the costs of buyers' agents

Professional buyers' agents and QPIAs provide a service for a fee. You need to understand what that service is as well as their specific investment strategy (because they generally have one) to ensure it fits in with your own personal real estate goals.

REMEMBER

You should expect to be charged a fee for the services provided by buyers' agents and QPIAs because they are professionals and deserve to be paid for their time and their advice. Some buyers' agents charge a percentage commission on the purchase price of the property they help you purchase, while others charge a flat fee for their services.

The most experienced operators provide a variety of services, including the following:

>> Finding and negotiating on a property in the area you'd like to live or, if investing, an area primed for future growth

>> Sourcing your new home based on your specific instructions

>> Preparing a property investment plan for you

>> Taking over the negotiation on a property that you have already located

WARNING

All of the options provided by buyers' agents are generally fee-for-service. If someone purporting to be a buyers' agent or advocate offers to undertake these services for free, you should be very wary, because they are being paid by someone, somewhere, and are likely not working for you independently at all.

REMEMBER

The top property investment professionals always disclose any commissions they might be paid — for example, for referrals to other people in the industry such as mortgage brokers. If they don't, or won't, you should question why.

Chapter **4**

Financing Your Property Purchase

Buying your first home or investment can seem like a daunting task that slips further and further from your grasp as you watch property prices climb ever higher. Nicola remembers feeling the same way in 2007 when she was trying to purchase her first property. (The $350,000 purchase price seemed horribly expensive when she was earning $60,000 a year and had a small deposit.) And that's the reality — saving the deposit for your first property has always been tricky because it takes time, effort and quite a significant commitment to budgeting.

But you don't have to be wealthy to begin making attractive real estate buying decisions. In this chapter, we present a wide range of funding options that offers something for virtually everyone's budget and personal situation.

Calculating the Costs of Entry

At some point in your life, you've surely had the experience of wanting to do something and then realising that you didn't have sufficient money to accomplish your goal. Perhaps it was as simple as lacking the change to buy a chocolate bar as a child. Or maybe it happened on a holiday when you ran low on funds and tried to do business with a shop owner who took only cash when you carried only a credit card. No matter — the world of real estate investing is no different. You can't play if you can't pay.

Determining what you need to get started

Most of the time, real estate buyers make a deposit and borrow most of the money needed to complete a purchase. That's the 'conventional way' to purchase properties, owner-occupied or investment, and is likely to be the most successful method for you in the long run (as it has been for us).

For most residential properties, including free-standing houses, semi-detached housing such as some townhouses and apartments, you can gain access to good financing terms by making at least a 10 per cent deposit or offering significant equity (if you already own a property), depending on your personal financial situation and the lending environment at the time.

WARNING

Most banks in Australia charge *lenders' mortgage insurance* (LMI) when the size of the deposit (or equity guarantee) is less than 20 per cent. LMI is an exponential charge that increases as the deposit offered by the property buyer decreases. For more about LMI, see 'Overcoming deposit limitations', later in this chapter.

REMEMBER

A minimum deposit of at least 10 per cent is recommended for first-time property buyers. You can escape being charged LMI if you have a deposit (or equity) of at least 20 per cent, but for most first-timers saving a 20 per cent deposit may be difficult.

You won't find such wonderful financing options for commercial real estate and vacant land. Compared with residential properties, these types of investments usually require larger deposits and/or higher interest rates and loan fees.

Determining how much cash you need to close on a purchase is largely a function of the estimated purchase price. Here's an example: If you're looking at buying a modest house priced at $800,000, a 20 per cent deposit equals $160,000. You then add another 4 to 6 per cent of the purchase price for settlement costs (including stamp duty, title-transfer fees, bank fees and legal fees) to reach the estimated deposit of $200,000 that you would need to get the best financing options. For a 10 per cent deposit (which is more likely for new property owners), the deposit could be around $120,000.

Most first home buyers will struggle to save a deposit of this magnitude, with many first-timers usually presenting a 5 to 10 per cent deposit as well as making the most of various state government grants and stamp duty concessions.

Don't forget stamp duty

After the actual cost of the property itself, the next biggest cost in buying properties in Australia is *land transfer duty* or *stamp duty* — a generally nasty, big, regressive tax levied by state and territory governments. Each government charges stamp duty in a different way, and it's usually tiered so that lower valued real estate is charged less stamp duty as a proportion of the value of the property. Investors often pay higher rates of stamp duty as well. For what reason, we're not sure.

Stamp duty usually ranges from about 3 to 5.5 per cent of the value of a property (although above certain amounts, it can be very close to 6 per cent). For example, buying a $650,000 established or new property in Victoria incurs a stamp duty of $34,070 if it's your home or principal place of residence — and if it's an investment property. If you're a first home buyer, you may qualify for a concession, which would result in a reduced stamp duty fee of $11,356.

However, in Queensland (which applies the cheapest stamp duty), buying a $650,000 property incurs a stamp duty of $15,100 for existing and new homeowners — however, this increases to $22,275 for investors.

TIP

For details of exactly how stamp duty is charged in your state or territory, contact your local state revenue office or department of treasury. The following list of website addresses can help you get started:

>> **Australian Capital Territory:** www.revenue.act.gov.au/duties

>> **New South Wales:** www.service.nsw.gov.au/

>> **Northern Territory:** www.nt.gov.au/employ/money-and-taxes

- » **Queensland:** www.treasury.qld.gov.au/budget-and-financial-management/revenue-and-taxation/
- » **South Australia:** www.revenuesa.sa.gov.au
- » **Tasmania:** www.sro.tas.gov.au/property-transfer-duties
- » **Victoria:** www.sro.vic.gov.au/land-transfer-duty
- » **Western Australia:** www.wa.gov.au/service/financial-management/taxation-and-duty

Overcoming deposit limitations

Many people, especially when they make their first real estate purchase, are strapped for cash. In order to qualify for the most attractive financing, lenders typically require that your deposit be at least 20 per cent of the property's purchase price. In addition, you need to reserve money to pay for other settlement costs such as stamp duty, title-transfer fees, and loan fees.

TIP

If you don't have 20-plus per cent of the purchase price, don't panic and don't get depressed — you can still own real estate. Here are some potential solutions:

- » **Lenders' mortgage insurance:** Most lenders can still offer you a mortgage even though you may be able to put down only 5 to 20 per cent of the purchase price. These lenders are likely to require you to pay lenders' mortgage insurance (LMI) for your loan. This insurance usually costs several thousands of dollars and is designed to protect the lender, not you, if you default on your loan. When you do have at least 20 per cent or higher equity in the property, you can usually eliminate the LMI.

- » **Delayed gratification:** If you don't want the cost and strain of extra fees and bad finance terms, postpone your purchase. Boost your savings. Examine your current spending habits and plan to build up a nest egg to use to invest in your first rental property. For more tips on saving, see the section 'Make saving a habit', later in this chapter.

- » **Thinking smaller:** Consider lower priced properties. Smaller properties and those that need some work can help keep down the purchase price. For example, a duplex where you live in one unit and rent out the other is also a cost-effective way to get started.

Rounding Up the Required Cash

Most successful real estate homebuyers and investors we know, including ourselves, started building their real estate investment portfolios the old-fashioned way — through saving money and then gradually buying properties over the years. Many people have difficulty saving money because they don't know how, or are simply unwilling, to limit their spending. Easy access to consumer debt (via credit cards, car loans and 'buy now, pay later' schemes, for example) creates huge obstacles to saving more and spending less — and many Australians holding credit cards don't pay off their debt in full each month. Buying and investing in real estate requires self-control, sacrifice and discipline. As with most good things in life, you must be patient and plan ahead to be able to purchase real estate.

Make saving a habit

As young adults, some people are naturally good savers. Those who save regularly have usually acquired good financial habits from their parents. Other good savers have a high level of motivation to accomplish goals — retiring young, starting a business, buying a home, prioritising time with their kids and so on. Achieving such goals is much harder (if not impossible) when you're living payday to payday and worried about next month's bills.

REMEMBER

If you're not satisfied with how much of your monthly earnings you're able to save, you have two options (and you can take advantage of both):

>> **Boost your income:** To increase your take-home pay, working more may be a possibility, or you may be able to take a more lucrative career path. But keep your priorities in order. Your personal health and relationships shouldn't be put on the backburner for a workaholic schedule. We also believe in investing in your education. A solid education is the path to greater financial rewards and can lead to all of the great goals we discuss here. Education isn't only a key to your chosen profession, but also to real estate purchasing and investing.

>> **Reduce your spending:** For most people, this is the path to increased savings. Start by analysing how much you spend on different areas (for example, food, clothing and

entertainment) each month. Then decide where and how you can cut back. Would you rather eat out less or have takeaway food delivered less often? How about driving a less expensive car versus taking lower cost holidays? Although the possibilities to reduce your spending are many, you and only you can decide which options you're willing and able to implement. If you need more help with this vital financial topic, a number of books and budgeting tools are available these days that can help guide you.

Tap into other cash sources

Saving money from your monthly earnings will probably be the foundation for your entry into your real estate purchasing program. However, you may have access to other financial resources for deposits.

As you gain more comfort and confidence as a real estate owner, you may wish to redirect some of your dollars from other investments — such as shares, bonds and managed funds — into property. If you do, be mindful of the following:

>> **Diversification:** Real estate is one of the prime investments (the others being shares and small business) for long-term appreciation potential. Be sure that you understand your portfolio's overall asset allocation and risk when making changes.

>> **Tax issues:** If you've held other investments for more than one year, you can take advantage of lower capital gains tax rates if you now wish to sell. The effective maximum federal government tax rate for long-term capital gains (investments sold for more than they were purchased for after more than 12 months) includes a 50 per cent reduction in the gain itself, for assets held longer than a year.

Primary Sources of Finance: Lenders Big and Small

When the Hawke–Keating federal government deregulated the banking system in the mid-1980s, the number of lenders in Australia exploded, as did the competition between them. At first, foreign banks rushed in, many of which later retreated or scaled back their activities after failing to understand the subtleties of the local market. But banks aren't the only institutions that now lend money for investment property in Australia. Alternative mainstream lenders include building societies, credit unions and non-bank lenders.

In the following sections, we describe the different types of mainstream lenders that you can approach to finance property investment, and briefly cover how they operate.

Banks

Traditionally, banks are deposit-taking institutions. They accept deposits from some customers and then lend this money to other customers. Because they're the backbone of the Australian financial system, banks are heavily regulated by federal government entities, including the Australian Prudential Regulatory Authority, the Australian Securities and Investments Commission, and the Reserve Bank of Australia.

When Australians think of banks, most call to mind the 'big four': The Australian and New Zealand Banking Group (ANZ, at www.anz.com), the Commonwealth Bank of Australia (CBA, at www.commbank.com.au), the National Australia Bank (NAB, at www.nab.com.au) and Westpac Banking Corporation (Westpac, at www.westpac.com.au). These banks are protected by the federal government's four pillars policy, which bans mergers between the four club members. And, between them, these banks account for more than 80 per cent of all loans from mortgage borrowers in Australia.

The big four aren't the only banks in Australia. Most states have at least one or two other banks, many of which are also expanding beyond their traditional state boundaries. These include the Bank of Queensland (www.boq.com.au) and Suncorp Bank (www.suncorp.com.au) in Queensland, Bendigo Bank (www.bendigobank.com.au) in Victoria, Banks SA (www.banksa.com.au) in South Australia, and BankWest (www.bankwest.com.au) in Western Australia (owned by the Commonwealth Bank of Australia).

The foreign banks with significant presences in Australia include HSBC (www.hsbc.com.au), Citibank (www.citibank.com.au) and ING (www.ing.com.au), to name just a few.

Building societies and credit unions

Prior to the mid-1980s, building societies and credit unions were the places you went to for a loan when the banks knocked you back. These institutions charged higher interest rates than the banks to cover the bigger risks they were taking to provide mortgages. They were also usually less efficient. These building societies and credit unions were traditionally operated as not-for-profit organisations to provide loans to their members.

Today, most building societies and credit unions offer interest rates that rival their larger banking competitors' rates and tend to differentiate themselves by providing customised service.

Non-bank lenders

The deregulation of the banking system in the 1980s eventually paved the way for non-bank lenders to become mainstream. The first and most successful of these was Aussie Home Loans (www. aussie.com.au), which arrived in time to ride the first big wave of anti-bank sentiment in the 1990s (generated by branch closures and sacking of staff to make higher profits) and undercut the banks' interest rates.

WARNING

As well as Aussie Home Loans, now called Aussie, other small and nimble providers have also entered the market to offer an array of loans in recent years. Some have the reputation of being a little fly-by-night, often appearing attractive because of very low interest rates. As a property buyer and investor, price shouldn't be everything in your decision of which lender to use, and using a well-established lender should be a priority.

The main difference between banks, building societies and credit unions on the one hand and non-bank lenders on the other is how they source the money they lend out to property buyers. The traditional lenders source their money from depositors, whereas the non-bank lenders tend to raise their money from international money markets — international investors seeking fixed-interest returns from reasonably secure investments, such as Australian mortgages.

Chapter **5**

Understanding Mortgages

Mortgages with a capital M — the word is enough to inspire financial fear in the uneducated. But here's the thing: Mortgages are nothing to be feared and rather should be seen as a vehicle for you to improve your financial future using other people's money — that is, the banks! You see, a mortgage on residential real estate is classed as *good debt* because your repayments are reducing the principal on a capital growth and, potentially, incoming-producing asset.

You probably also have questions about how to select the mortgage that's most appropriate for the property you're buying and your overall personal and financial situation. This chapter covers the financing options you should consider (and highlights those you should avoid).

Taking a Look at Mortgages

Although you can find thousands of different types of mortgages (thanks to all the various bells and whistles available), you need to understand the four basic mortgage types, covered in two groups. The first group focuses on the type of interest rates you can choose — *variable* interest rates or *fixed* interest rates. The second group involves a decision on whether your repayments will be *interest-only* or also repay part of the borrowed capital, called a *principal and interest* (P&I) loan. All mortgages combine at least one element from the first group — variable or fixed interest — with one from the second group — interest-only or P&I repayments. But mortgages can combine both elements of each group — the interest rates can remain fixed for a number of years and then have a variable interest rate after that, and the repayments can start off as interest-only and then later switch to principal and interest. In the following sections, we discuss these major loan types, what features they typically have and how you can intelligently compare them with each other and select the one that best fits with your property purchase.

Going with the flow: Variable-rate mortgages

The vast majority of all mortgages taken out in Australia — whether for investment purposes or to buy your own home — are taken out as variable-rate mortgages, usually for terms of 25 or 30 years (although some lenders are now offering 40-year terms). Variable-rate mortgages carry an interest rate that changes over time, usually tracking the changes made by the Reserve Bank of Australia (RBA) to the 'official cash rate'. In fact, for more than the 15 years before the GFC, whatever change the RBA made to the cash rate was matched equally by the major lenders. However, lenders' 'costs of financing' changed dramatically following the GFC and banks no longer move in lock step with the RBA. The RBA can commonly make, say, a cut of 0.5 percentage points, but the banks then only pass on 0.3 or 0.4 percentage points. And when the RBA has increased rates by, say, 0.25 percentage points, the banks have sometimes increased their rates by 0.3 or 0.4 percentage points.

A variable-rate mortgage starts with a set interest rate, but can move up or down each and every month during the course of a 25- or 30-year mortgage. In practice, variable rates tend to move probably only a few times each year. Because a variable interest rate changes over time, so, too, does the size of the loan's monthly repayment. Variable rates are attractive for a number of reasons:

>> At most points of the interest rates cycle, variable rates are lower than fixed rates. So, given the economics of a typical investment property purchase, variable rates are more likely to enable you to achieve positive cash flow in the early years of property ownership.

>> Should interest rates decline, you can realise most, if not all, of the benefits of lower rates without the cost and hassle of refinancing. With a fixed-rate mortgage (which we discuss next), the only way to benefit from an overall decline in the market level of interest rates is to refinance, which can result in expensive exit fees from your current loan.

Depending on the individual lender's policies, variable-rate loans usually come with many more features and options than do fixed-rate mortgages. But variable rates also come in two broad types — standard and discount variable rates.

Standard variable rates

The standard variable rate (SVR) is generally a lender's full-service loan product. Although it has a different name at almost every banking institution, SVR is the figure most often quoted by the media when they talk about mortgage interest rates, or rising or falling interest rates. The SVR is usually the highest rate charged to general mortgage customers, but often comes with other products thrown in, which can be useful to some customers, such as offset accounts, redraw accounts and fee-free general banking.

But, despite the fact that the SVR is the most often quoted interest rate, few customers actually pay it. Customers — particularly property investors, who tend to have higher average total loan balances — find that most banks discount the offered interest rate from the SVR.

Discount variable rates and 'no frills' loans

Discount variable rates are in essence SVR loans with a discount applied to them.

REMEMBER

Generally speaking, you should be able to receive a discounted rate to the SVR — unless you have recently rolled off a fixed rate and didn't request a discount or, potentially, you forgot to pay your package fee and lost the package benefits, which include discounts off the SVR.

The advertised discount on the SVR is usually between 0.70 and 1.30 per cent across the lenders. However, these amounts are the *minimum* that will be offered with packaged products — and certainly not the maximum. In fact, they can be negotiated on request and the discounts that can be achieved are on average twice as high as the advertised discount.

Also available are 'no frills' loans that may be attractive to some borrowers at the start of their purchasing or investment journeys. Generally, these loans won't offer access to products such as offset accounts, redraw accounts and fee-free banking.

These lower rate products may suit you when you're starting out with your first, relatively low value, property. However, even if you're buying a more expensive first property, a bank, if asked, will offer all the extras available with a standard variable rate, but at an interest rate normally associated with a discounted loan.

TIP

The basic or 'no frills' loans may offer lower rates than the standard SVR; however, don't just use this as your comparison rate. You should be able to negotiate having access to the SVR products while still receiving a discounted rate. The basic loans are usually offered with a rate that's approximately an additional 0.20 to 0.60 per cent lower than the SVR rates with the advertised discounts. But you're often able to negotiate the SVR discount further, ending up with a discount SVR rate that's the same or lower than the basic product rate (depending on total loan size and other factors).

Honeymoon rates

Lenders often offer an introductory rate for a mortgage, known as *honeymoon* or *introductory* rates. These rates usually offer a discount of about 0.60 to 1.20 per cent. Don't be fooled, though: You won't pay this tantalisingly low rate for very long. These rates are inevitably offered for periods of as short as six months, or as long as two years. This rate is referred to as a honeymoon rate because the lower initial interest rate gives the borrower a gentle easing-in to the longer term costs of a mortgage.

REMEMBER

The introductory rate is often set artificially low to entice you into the product. In other words, even if the market level of interest rates doesn't change, your variable-rate mortgage is destined to increase at the end of the defined honeymoon period.

Crucially, you need to know what your interest rate will 'revert' to when, as they say, the honeymoon is over. What's the point in having a low introductory rate if you're just going to have to repay those 'savings' and more when you change to the higher rate? Saving $500 now only to have to repay $1,000 or $2,000 six or 12 months later is rarely (probably never) going to make sense. And the 'extras' might come not just in the form of higher interest, but higher fees and charges. In most cases, the honeymoon rate will revert to a standard variable rate (refer to 'Standard variable rates', earlier in this chapter).

Concerns over borrowers being duped by low honeymoon rates has reduced dramatically since the introduction in recent years of average annual percentage rates (AAPR), under the general principle of 'truth in advertising', by lenders.

Average annual percentage rates

Much more important than an artificially low introductory interest rate is the average cost of the loan over a given period — that is, if the rate is cheaper at the start and more expensive later, what's the average cost over, say, seven years?

This concern over borrowers being seduced or duped by low introductory rates led some industry figures and state governments to introduce the concept of average annual percentage rates (AAPRs) to interest-rate advertising by Australian lenders. The AAPR, also sometimes referred to as a comparison rate or a true rate, is designed to force lenders to bundle all of the associated costs of a loan — such as interest rates, fees and charges — and average them over a seven-year period for the purpose of advertising the 'true' cost of the mortgage. This bundling creates an average interest rate that makes it easier for customers to compare rates offered by various lenders — and to realise that a honeymoon rate, for example, might not be such a great deal.

What does this mean for potential borrowers? It means you'll often see an interest rate advertised for a product with a different comparison rate alongside it. Almost inevitably, the lower rate is the loan's advertised interest rate. The higher figure is likely to be the AAPR rate, or the one that takes in the cost of the lower introductory rate, the higher ongoing rate, plus the other bank fees and charges due over the course of a seven-year period.

For example, a one-year honeymoon rate (refer to the preceding section) may have an advertised rate of 3.6 per cent, and an AAPR of 3.96 per cent. As another example, a two-year honeymoon rate may be 3.74 per cent, versus an AAPR of 4.46 per cent.

REMEMBER

Finding a loan with the lowest AAPR isn't necessarily the most important factor in determining which loan is best for you. Loans may have low AAPRs because they don't have some other loan functions that you may want or need. The AAPR is just one way to compare a part of one loan with another.

The security of fixed-rate mortgages

Less common than variable-rate mortgages in Australia, fixed-rate mortgages tend to be offered for periods of between one and ten years, depending on the individual lender. The interest rate remains constant over the life of the agreed loan term. Because the interest rate stays the same, your monthly mortgage payment stays the same.

For the purpose of making future estimates of your property's costs (and, if an investment property, its cash flow), fixed-rate mortgages can offer you certainty and some peace of mind for fixed periods, because you know precisely the size of your mortgage payment next month, next year and up to ten years from now. (Of course, the other costs of owning property — such as property insurance and maintenance — will still escalate over the years.)

Peace of mind has a price, though. The following points examine some of the conditions of fixed-rate mortgages:

TIP

>> Fixed-rate loans are usually inflexible. Many lenders won't let you make extra repayments or, if they do, only under restricted conditions. Should you find that you need to sell your property — and, therefore, don't need the loan anymore — you might find that you face hefty exit fees.

>> Depending on the stage of the credit cycle, with fixed rates you normally pay a premium in the form of a higher interest rate, compared with loans that have a variable interest rate over time. In other words, you're paying a premium for your 'peace of mind'.

>> If the property is an investment and if, like most investment property buyers, you're facing a tough time generating a healthy positive cash flow in the early years of owning the property, a fixed-rate mortgage may make it even more financially challenging. A variable-rate mortgage, by contrast, can lower your property's carrying costs in those early years. (Refer to the section 'Going with the flow: Variable-rate mortgages', earlier in this chapter.)

>> Fixed-rate loans carry the risk that, if interest rates fall significantly after you obtain your mortgage and you're unable to refinance, you're stuck with a relatively higher cost mortgage until the loan term completes its fixed period. Also remember that, even if you're able to refinance, you'll probably spend a significant sum in exit fees and new loan fees by doing so. Many borrowers who had fixed rate mortgages before the COVID19 pandemic missed out on once-in-a-lifetime low interest rates, for example.

REMEMBER

While fixed rates can increase your property's carrying costs, they can be invaluable if the interest rates are locked in at a low point of the interest rate cycle. If, for example, you've locked in a rate of 3 per cent and then interest rates rise, say, two to three percentage points (as they did in 2022 as Australia emerged from the COVID-19 pandemic), you have a very cheap source of financing until your locked-in period finishes.

Tax-effective interest-only loans

Many Australians have been brought up with a fear of debt. From the time many of us start to learn about money, it's rammed into our heads that when you get a loan (for any purpose), your primary goal is to get that loan repaid as quickly as possible. In the extreme, some people believe you should put your enjoyment of life itself on hold until the loan is repaid. But buying property — be it a home or an investment — almost inevitably requires borrowed money. And, although it may shock you to hear this, in some cases, it makes financial sense to never actually pay the bank its money back! Just pay interest — that is, rent the bank's money — forever.

This might particularly be the case if you're borrowing to buy property as an investment. Australia's tax laws at the time of writing state that interest paid on money borrowed to fund investments is tax-deductible, whereas repayment of investment capital and personal, non-investment debt is not deductible. So, if you have an interest-only loan on an investment property, in most cases, all of your interest costs qualify as a tax deduction. However, if you repay some of the original money you borrowed, that portion of repaid capital does not qualify as a deduction. All repayment of money for personal loans (including your home, cars, holidays and credit cards) is also not deductible against your other income.

Whether the loan interest is tax-deductible or not is the basis of what is often referred to as the *good debt/bad debt* principle. If you have a number of loans, some of which are investment (good debt) and some of which are personal (bad debt), then you should always aim to pay off the bad debt before attacking repayment of any of the good debt. The only exception may be if the interest rate on the good debt was significantly higher than the rate on your bad debt (which is rarely, if ever, the case with investment property).

TECHNICAL STUFF

Here's an example of the good debt/bad debt principle: Assume an investment property loan of $600,000, with an interest rate of 4.5 per cent. If the loan is interest-only, the repayments required each year will be $27,000. Under most circumstances (assuming that the property is rented or available for rent) and with most investment properties, that entire $27,000 will be a tax deduction. However, if the same loan is a 25-year principal and interest (P&I) loan, the annual repayment in the first year will be about $40,000. Of that sum, $27,000 will be interest and $13,000 will be repayment of principal and won't be deductible. Only the $27,000 will be a tax deduction. Although no difference exists between the two sums that qualify as a deduction, the investor still has to find more than $13,000 extra each year for repayment of principal that he won't have to find on an interest-only loan.

'But at least the loan is being repaid!' is the reaction of many to suggestions that people not aim to repay principal quickly. If this is the only loan that an investor has, an interest-only loan might not be an option, as many lenders may insist on principal being repaid. And nothing is wrong with repaying loan principal, because it will need to be repaid in some way at some point in time. However, it's not always the most tax-effective solution for an investor. In particular, if investors who have other non-deductible debt accelerate payments on their personal debt, they're usually better off in two ways. Most investors have some money owing on their own home. By focusing repayment of principal onto the home loan, the investor is both minimising the non-deductible interest on the home loan and maximising tax-deductible interest payments on the investment loan.

To take the previous example one step further, if the investor uses that $13,000 to pay down his own home loan, he'll save interest on the home loan (which would compound the following year).

REMEMBER

Some lenders only insist on principal being repaid from one of their loans. If you have a home loan and an investment property loan (or many investment property loans) with the same lender, the lender may want you to repay principal on the home loan, but allow long-term, interest-only repayments on the remainder — until such time as the home loan is paid off, when the lender will generally want to convert one of the other interest-only investment loans to principal and interest (P&I).

The downside of interest-only loans is that the amount of money owed against the property doesn't fall. If you buy a property with a $600,000 loan, after three years of interest-only repayments, you'll still owe the bank $600,000.

Making a dent with principal and interest loans

For a principal and interest (P&I) loan, the borrower agrees to pay the lender not only the interest on the loan but also some of the initial capital each week, fortnight or month. Over the term of the loan, which usually starts at 25 or 30 years for mortgages in Australia, the initial sum borrowed is repaid in full and the mortgage comes to an end.

Apart from the effect of changes to official interest rates, P&I loan repayment amounts are constant throughout the term of the loan. What changes during that period is the amount of money within that repayment that's assigned as interest and the amount that's designated as repayment of capital. The reduction in the principal component of the loan is worked out by a mathematical formula known as *amortisation*. Initially, the majority of the repayment is designated as interest repayments and a small amount is to repay the initial capital, or principal. And as the principal gets paid down, the amount of interest reduces, and the amount used to pay off principal increases.

TECHNICAL STUFF

Here's an example: A 25-year, $600,000 principal and interest loan with a 4.5 per cent interest rate will require repayments of about $3,334 a month. In the first month of repayment, $2,250 will go towards interest and about $1,084 will be repayment of principal. At the end of the first year, the amount being directed to interest versus principal repayment won't have changed very much — $2,204 will be interest and $1,130 will go towards principal. However, at the end of the 12th year, the $3,334 will be split as $1,481 for interest and $1,853 for principal. The final repayment, when the loan is finally paid out, will be $12.46 in interest and $3,322 as the last principal repayment.

An owner has two ways to increase the amount of equity in a property. The first is that the value of the property itself increases; the second is that the value of the loan decreases. P&I loans are one option where home owners can exercise control in increasing their equity ownership in a property.

Making Some Decisions

You can't (or at least shouldn't) spend months deciding which mortgage may be right for your situation. You can also work with professional mortgage brokers to undertake most of this research for you. However, in the following sections, we help you zero in on which type of mortgage may be best for you.

Deciding between variable and fixed

Choosing between a variable-rate and a fixed-rate loan is an important decision in the real estate purchasing process. Consider the advantages and disadvantages of each mortgage type and decide what's best for your situation prior to refinancing or purchasing real estate.

How much risk can you handle in regard to the size of your property's monthly mortgage payment? If you can take the financial risks that come with a variable rate — the main risk being that your mortgage could rise considerably if the Reserve Bank, or your bank, raises interest rates — you have a better chance of saving money and, if an investor, maximising your property's cash flow with a variable-rate rather than a fixed-rate loan. Variable interest rates tend to start lower and stay lower, if the overall level of interest rates stays unchanged. Even if rates go up, they'll likely come back down over the life of your loan. If you stick with a variable loan for better and for worse, you should come out ahead in the long run.

Variable rates make more sense if you borrow less than you're qualified for. If your income (and, if applicable, your investment property cash flow) significantly exceeds your spending, you may feel less anxiety about a fluctuating interest rate. If you do choose a variable loan, you may feel more secure if you have a sizeable financial cushion of a few months' expenses reserved, which you can access if rates go up.

WARNING

Some people take variable rates without thoroughly understanding whether they can really afford them. When rates rise, property owners who can't afford higher payments can face a financial crisis. If you don't have emergency savings you can tap into to make the higher payments, how can you afford the monthly payments and the other expenses of your property? Bank loan approval processes generally build in a buffer when trying to determine whether a borrower can afford to meet higher repayments, in case interest rates rise. If interest rates at the time of an application were 5 per cent, for example, the bank would generally want to be satisfied that the customer could meet repayments if interest rates were to rise to 7 or 8 per cent. The banks' system is obviously not foolproof, and smaller or less scrupulous lenders may not be as diligent in assessing a customer's repayment power before approving a loan.

REMEMBER

Over the longer term, variable-rate mortgages tend to be cheaper (because the investors making their money available for banks to lend on fixed terms expect a higher rate to lock their money away). But don't ignore fixed-rate mortgages. If you see a fixed rate that you believe is affordable and may allow you to sleep more soundly at night, consider locking in that rate for a term.

Some property people recommend locking in for a long time if you find a suitable rate, whereas others believe it's best to fix rates for only short periods when you believe the market has temporarily mispriced the likely future interest rate movements.

TECHNICAL STUFF

Fixed interest rates tend to reflect the level that lenders believe rates are heading towards over the fixed rate term. If investors believe that interest rates are likely to fall over the next couple of years, one-and two-year fixed rates may be lower than some variable interest rates. If they believe that interest rates are heading up, fixed rates may be higher than variable rates. You also can have short- and long-term fixed rates on different sides of current variable rates. If investors believe that the Reserve Bank is likely to cut interest rates over the short term (possibly to add extra stimulus to the economy) but raise them in the medium to long term, one-, two- and three-year fixed rates may be below current variable rates, while five-, seven- and ten-year rates may be above. This scenario can also work in the reverse.

TIP

You may also consider a split loan, which combines features of variable- and fixed-rate mortgages. Most major lenders allow borrowers to choose to fix a percentage of their home loan and have the rest of the loan as variable. This apportionment is designed to give the borrower partial protection against future interest rate rises. If rates do rise, only half your mortgage will require higher repayments. The opposite applies if rates fall, where you may be stuck paying a higher interest rate on the fixed portion of your loan.

Deciding between interest-only and principal and interest

If you're purchasing property as an investor, the decision on whether to take an interest-only or principal and interest (P&I) loan should be a simple one. If you have other non-deductible debt (such as a home loan, car loan or personal loan), it usually makes more financial sense to take out an interest-only loan for your investment property. Any savings should be redirected to repaying the principal on loans that can't be claimed as a tax deduction, particularly your principal place of residence (refer to 'Tax-effective interest-only loans', earlier in this chapter).

However, many homebuyers and investors won't feel comfortable with an interest-only loan, and that's okay. Repaying principal on any loan — investment or otherwise — is a good thing. It's just not as tax-effective for investors because the repaid principal can't be claimed as a tax deduction.

Some other investors — young people buying an investment property before buying their first home and older people who've paid off their home — won't have any non-deductible debt and may want to repay the principal on their investment loan as a way of building equity faster, but this may mean they are unable to add to their portfolio as quickly as they may have done otherwise.

Deciding on a loan term

Most mortgage lenders offer you the option of 25-year or 30-year mortgages. Borrowers can also ask for shorter loan terms if they want, but rarely do so. So, how do you decide whether a shorter or longer term mortgage is best for your investment property purchase?

The difference in repayments between 25- and 30-year loan terms isn't significant. On a $600,000 loan at 4.5 per cent, a 25-year term would have P&I monthly repayments of approximately $3,334, whereas a 30-year term would have $3,040. This decision is often a function of whether you choose to pay interest-only or P&I. If you choose P&I because you'd rather repay your debt faster, you may also want a shorter term.

TIP

If you decide on a 30-year mortgage over a 25-year mortgage, or a 25-year mortgage over a 20-year mortgage, you may still maintain the flexibility to pay the mortgage off faster if you choose to. You can make larger payments than necessary and create your own 25- or 20-year mortgage. You can also fall back to making only the payments required on the original schedule when the need arises. Some loans, usually fixed-rate loans, have restrictions on prepayments and may charge a fee for early repayment of capital. We dislike mortgages with *pre-payment penalties* (penalties for paying off your loan before you're supposed to). Normally, pre-payment penalties don't apply if you pay off a loan because you sell the property, but when you refinance a loan that has pre-payment penalties, you have to pay the penalty. And while the Australian Government moved to ban exit fees on home loans many years ago, exceptions to the rules always occur — so make sure you find out what exit fees your lender charges ahead of finally making the decision to pay out the loan.

Sizing Up Banking Products

Literally thousands of mortgage products and options are on offer, and hundreds of lenders, some of which offer dozens of combinations of loans each. How on earth are you supposed to find the perfect one for you? Relax. You probably won't find the perfect one. The best thing to do is make sure the loan you settle on suits you and your situation and offers a level of service you find acceptable.

The starting point for finding a suitable loan is to find out about the basic products and whether or not you need or want them.

Interest rates: Is cheaper always better?

Whether you're a homebuyer or investor, if you're paying P&I most of your repayments at the start of your loan will be covering interest costs. (Refer to the section 'Making a dent with principal and interest loans', earlier in the chapter, for more on this.) For investors, the biggest ongoing cost of property investment is usually the interest being paid on the loan. That is almost certainly the case in the early stages of an investment if you use a loan to fund most of your purchase. So, for owner-occupiers or investors, putting in the groundwork to find a good relationship and a cheap source of funding makes sense.

The sharp increase in the number of lenders since the mid-1980s has meant a considerable increase in competition. Competition was good for borrowers on two main fronts. The first was that competition put a major squeeze on interest rate margins — making loans considerably cheaper — and the second was that the variety of lending products expanded dramatically.

REMEMBER

The global financial crisis (GFC) put an end to the interest rate squeeze suffered by banks, which had been so wonderful for consumers. Interest rate margins — the difference between the interest rate banks pay to get the money and the rate at which they lend it out — have been increasing since early 2008. The foundation of the GFC was actually a global credit crisis and those lending the credit to banks to on-lend to borrowers started demanding two things. First, they wanted higher rates paid for their credit. Second, they wanted less risk. Both of those demands then increased the cost of funding to the banks, which was passed on in the form of higher interest rates to consumers.

The cheapest source of funding isn't necessarily always the best source of funding. Usually, the cheaper the interest rate on a loan, the fewer bells and whistles attached. Nothing is wrong with hunting down the cheapest investment loan rate when you're sourcing a property — for your home or as an investment — but you may find that a product with a slightly higher interest rate may save you money in the long run.

Most lenders can quote a range of interest rates, which often only serves to confuse potential customers, but generally speaking the SVR with a discount applied is the most common.

Merging your home and investment finances

Most people approaching their first investment property have already bought their own home and probably still have a home loan. Taking on extra investment debt can have advantages — you might find that banks are keener to keep you, or lure you, with lower interest rates or extra products that may be useful in your personal life, such as free credit cards, redraw and offset accounts or rewards programs.

Few banks offer particularly rewarding discounts if you have loans of less than $250,000. So, the addition of an investment property mortgage — which will usually be more than $600,000 these days — may give you loans of more than $850,000. If you have two investment properties and your own home, for example, then it's reasonable to assume that your total aggregate lending is $1 million or more, which would attract the largest discounts. A mortgage broker can be vital in securing the best discounts for you in this scenario (refer to the section 'The rise of mortgage brokers', earlier in this chapter).

Having $1 million or more in aggregate lending will make you considerably more appealing to a lender. Previously you may have been paying full price on a standard variable loan and the associated frills, or have been on a discount variable rate, without the benefits. With most banks, if you're about to sign up for an additional investment property mortgage, you only have to ask in order to get all the benefits of a standard variable loan for the price of a discount variable loan — or get your mortgage broker to do the heavy lifting for you.

TECHNICAL STUFF

Here's an example of how increasing your debt can give your bank an incentive to lower your interest rate: You may have been paying a standard variable interest rate of 4 per cent for a $600,000 loan. But the addition of a $600,000 investment property loan gives you $1.2 million of total business with the bank. You could rightly expect to see your interest rate cut by up to 0.15 to 0.40 percentage points, depending on the lending environment at the time. Although this is obviously good news for the investment property loan, the interest on your home loan has just fallen as well.

Chapter **6**

Working Out the Ongoing Costs of Real Estate

When you buy residential real estate, you must do so with the knowledge that costs will be ongoing throughout your ownership period. That's because — unlike shares, for example — property is a depreciating asset, which means that it will need regular maintenance and repairs to ensure it stays in tip-top shape. Plus, you have to pay a variety of expenses to various entities, such as rates to your local council. Of course, for investors, if you have chosen wisely, your rent should ultimately cover all the standard expenses. And all property owners should have insurance to help fund major repairs when and if they arise.

Ongoing costs are part and parcel of property buying and investment. Although for investors the income stream from property (rent) is usually fairly even, the expenses side of the equation is less so. Some bills come monthly or quarterly. Some can be annual. But plenty of bills can come crashing down out of nowhere. And they simply must be paid. Taking the 'lumpy' nature of property costs into account when putting together your finances — either as an owner-occupier or investor — can save plenty of heartache down the track. From the mortgage to maintenance and body corporate fees, to ongoing property taxes, utility charges, agents' fees, property improvements and even insurance — this chapter tells you about the range of property costs that you might need to budget for.

Budgeting for the Inevitable

Managing real estate — even if that real estate is your home — is a slimmed-down version of managing your own business. If you've bought the property on your own or with your spouse (which is how most property is bought, although more and more people are buying when they are single or even investing independently from their partners), then your property is your asset, and you need to be involved in making the decisions. For investors, some of the decisions are small and can be left to people you employ, if you so wish, but some decisions are major, and you wouldn't want anyone else to make them for you.

As an investor, even if you've employed a property manager to do much of the work for you and an accountant to do some other parts of the work for you, they will always come back to you when the big decisions need to be made. The big decisions are inevitably about big costs — particularly where an item has given up the ghost and must be replaced.

In the following sections, we cover some of the expenses you need to budget for.

Mortgage interest — month in, month out

For most property owners, the single biggest ongoing expense is the interest on the mortgage, certainly in the first few years if most of the purchase price was financed with a loan. In many cases, for investors, this expense alone can soak up all the rent received and some of your personal income. The good news is that interest paid on money borrowed is, in most cases, tax-deductible for investors, meaning that it can be claimed against your income.

Interest costs are also one of the few costs that are likely to fluctuate significantly from year to year. Interest costs are linked to the cash rate set by the Reserve Bank of Australia (RBA). If the RBA is lifting rates because it's trying to control inflation or because the economy is picking up strength, interest costs can increase significantly. Conversely, if inflation is considered to be low or benign — or there is a worldwide health pandemic — and the RBA is concerned about the economy slowing too much, rates can fall fairly quickly. (Refer to Chapter 5 for more on interest rates.)

TECHNICAL
STUFF

For all the media interest and focus on the issue, the RBA doesn't change interest rates all that often — unless significant global events are affecting the market dramatically. During the global financial crisis and the COVID19 pandemic, for example, cash rates dropped in rapid succession to protect national economies from the financial fallout as much as possible.

Over the course of any property loan held for longer than a year, interest rates will both rise and fall. If your loan is for an investment property, keep track of your account statements, because making sure you claim your legal entitlements to costs such as interest expenses is a considerable factor in determining the financial success of your investment.

Financing unpredictable maintenance issues

Question: How can you plan for a heating or cooling system conking out? A toilet that now refuses to flush? Or for a keyhole rusting over? How about burst water pipes? **Answer:** You can't really. Whether you've previously lived in your parents' home, a rental property, or a home you bought and have lived in for some time, you probably have firsthand experience that property-maintenance issues are unpredictable at best and, at worst, perfectly timed to cause maximum financial distress.

Usually, when looking after your first property, most maintenance issues aren't going to become obvious until they've actually gone beyond the 'maintenance' stage and are on to the 'repair or replace' stage. Some maintenance issues can be looked at semi-regularly to ensure you keep on top of them.

TIP

One way of finding out where some maintenance issues or structural problems may be hiding, especially before you buy a property, is to hire a professional builder to conduct a pre-purchase inspection report. A building expert is able to point out major faults and potential structural-maintenance issues that could, or should, be looked at over the short term — one, two or three years. In some instances, the report may sway you against buying that property at all or could give you leverage to negotiate the final purchase price. But even the experts can't predict the remaining life span of some of the bigger and important items.

When discussing financing regular property costs and 'lumpy' property costs, the biggest concern for a first-time property owner is 'How much do I need to have available for these sorts of emergencies?' Unfortunately, no simple answer is possible. However, you can use the following list to help figure out what you may need:

>> **Is the house old or new?** Older period-style houses are understandably likely to be more expensive to maintain, because more of the items in them are older and closer to getting to the end of their use-by date.

>> **Has the property been renovated recently?** Especially for older properties, does it look like the current owner has been doing work to update the property? If the house has things such as freshly polished floorboards, a new garden, or an updated bathroom, kitchen or laundry, it's possible they got a contractor to fix up a few other problems at the same time.

>> **Are the fixtures and fittings in the house old?** Have a look at items such as ovens, toilets, air conditioners, gas heaters, exhaust fans, hot-water systems and household taps to see how well they've been maintained or how recently they've been replaced.

One of the most important things you can do is ask questions. If you're buying the property to move straight into or lease out to tenants immediately — that is, you're not buying the property to renovate or to knock it down and rebuild — ask the agent selling the property to find out when major structural work was last done or when things were last attended to. Not relevant for every property but, if necessary, ask about restumping, rewiring, reroofing and replumbing. When were these jobs done and by whom?

TIP

Here's a good standard for first-time property owners: Set aside or, at the very least, ensure you can easily access about $5,000 to fund small emergency maintenance or structural work.

WARNING

Be aware of tax implications that may also apply to maintaining your property if you are an investor. The Australian Taxation Office (ATO) has specific rules about what an investor can claim deductions for in the first year of ownership. The rules are designed to restrict obvious maintenance costs from effectively being passed on to the taxpayer. In some cases, early repairs and maintenance may need to be treated as a capital expense and depreciated over a number of years, rather than claimed as an up-front deduction.

Real estate agent management of maintenance costs

If you're purchasing the property as an investment and a real estate agent will be managing your property, be aware that most basic rental agreements usually give the agent the authority to approve urgent repairs up to a pre-determined limit. This arrangement is to cover most true emergencies that affect the ongoing enjoyment of the property by the tenant — hot-water systems breaking down, problems with heating or cooling systems and leaking pipes or toilets, for example. In most cases, the property manager uses a contractor, who bills the agent, and then the real estate agent bills you. If the work is less than the rent the agent collects for you each month, in most cases the agent will take the charge out of your next month's rent and pass on any remaining rent as normal.

Funding major maintenance issues

Bigger and more expensive maintenance work is not uncommon for many property purchases. If a particularly expensive problem emerges — such as the realisation that the roof really must be replaced immediately or the bathroom, kitchen or laundry needs to be renovated before you can move in or lease the property out to tenants — then it could be time to go to the bank to get funding.

Body corporate fees

Most apartments or units are governed by a *body corporate* or *owners corporation* (to an extent determined by the laws of the state in which the property is located), comprised of all owners of individual units within the block.

Several laws govern the existence of bodies corporate, designed to cover everything from blocks of several hundred apartments to a subdivided property with joint use of land. The main purpose of a body corporate is to take control of the maintenance of common property, usually the external areas of the buildings and shared grounds and facilities, and issues that affect many or all of the owners of properties that are adjoined or share a building lot. Some bodies corporate simply get together once a year to determine if any issues exist that require a vote. Legal requirements vary from state to state for the responsibilities of a body corporate but, normally, a body corporate must have a committee, hold committee meetings and an annual general meeting, and ensure that the public liability insurance for common areas is up to date.

One of the main duties of a body corporate is to look after joint maintenance issues — such as gardening, external painting and cleaning. These items are paid for through funds, via quarterly fees, raised from the owners of the properties. The day-to-day maintenance issues are usually covered by a body corporate administration fund. Most complexes also have a building or sinking fund for major capital works.

In most cases, both of these funds require regular contributions from owners so that enough money is available to deal with maintenance issues over time. Regular contributions are put aside so that major maintenance projects can be attended to when required or scheduled.

WARNING

Before you buy a property that may have a body corporate attached to it, make sure you find out the exact status of its finances. Also, make sure you read the body's governing document. Bodies corporate that have administration funds or building/sinking funds that are broke, that have trouble collecting dues from their owners or have a long list of items that look like they should have been attended to some time ago could be a warning to keep clear of the property. Before buying in, find out exactly what you'll be required to pay each quarter or each year, and any work that has been planned and costed that will require you to put your hand in your pocket. Some body corporate items still come out of the blue but, by doing your research, you may be able to reduce the impact of unexpected financial shocks.

Ongoing Property Taxes

Governments at all levels have their fingers all over real estate. A few big taxes are levied up-front, such as stamp duty to state governments and the 10 per cent GST on property construction to the federal government. And, of course, you have annual income tax return commitments as an investor, too. But you'll also find a few other less well-known taxes that you may need to pay regularly and should be aware of.

Council rates

Rates are levied by individual local councils and shires across Australia to pay for services provided to residents, such as rubbish collection, the building of footpaths and bicycle tracks, street cleaning, parking management, tree trimming, the maintenance of public gardens and traffic maintenance (which are important to the upkeep of your house and your street). Rates can also contribute to local services and community organisations, such as parents' groups, senior citizens' groups, libraries and family care centres (all of which may be of interest to you or your tenants). Unlike stamp duty and land tax, discussed in the next section, at least you get something directly in return from ongoing council rates. In some states, councils or council-run bodies are also the providers of some utility services, including water, drainage and sewerage (for more information on these services, see 'Utility charges', later in this chapter).

Every council has its own method of determining the actual rate to be levied on individual properties. In most cases, the amount is worked out according to the value of the property — that is, higher value properties pay proportionately more in council rates than lower value properties.

WARNING

Rates are usually levied quarterly, half-yearly or annually in advance. How those rates can be paid is determined by individual councils. A previous owner has likely paid council rates in advance, covering a proportion of the post-settlement period, requiring the new property owner to reimburse the previous owner for that expense. The amount owing is usually calculated during the conveyancing process and the payment made during the settlement process.

Land tax

Land tax is another charge levied by state governments and the Australian Capital Territory. At the time of writing, the Northern Territory doesn't have a land tax. Like stamp duty, no obvious or direct benefit flows on to the person being charged the tax. Land tax is a regressive wealth tax designed to target property investors specifically. To that end, land tax is usually not levied on a person's principal place of residence (the family home) but is levied on all other landholdings within a state.

Land tax is an annual tax that's charged differently in every state. In some states, it's not levied until a property investor has land valued above a specified amount. When that ceiling has been breached, land tax then becomes payable on the value of all remaining land held by the investor in that state. The land value under that limit is never taxed. And that's an important point. Land tax is levied on the value of the land held by the investor, not the value of the property (which includes buildings and capital improvements) itself.

TIP

For details of exactly how land tax is charged in your state or territory, contact your local state revenue office or department of treasury. The following list of website addresses can help you get started:

>> **Australian Capital Territory:** www.revenue.act.gov.au/land-tax

>> **New South Wales:** www.revenue.nsw.gov.au/taxes-duties-levies-royalties/land-tax

>> **Queensland:** www.treasury.qld.gov.au/budget-and-financial-management/revenue-and-taxation/

>> **South Australia:** www.revenuesa.sa.gov.au

>> **Tasmania:** www.sro.tas.gov.au/land-tax

>> **Victoria:** www.sro.vic.gov.au/land-tax

>> **Western Australia:** www.wa.gov.au/organisation/department-of-finance/land-tax

As an investor, you can't do a lot to escape land tax if you're investing in one state or territory and own a number of investment properties. With rising land values around the nation, land tax can be many tens of thousands of dollars per year but it's important to understand that you do normally need a reasonably sized portfolio for land tax to kick in. That means that most investors — who generally own just one or two properties — may never have to pay much land tax or pay it at all.

WARNING

In 2022, the Queensland Government passed legislation to take into account your total holdings across Australia when working out the land tax to be paid on your holdings in the Sunshine State. (Land tax was to be calculated on your total holdings, and then a percentage charged based on how much of this total was made up of holdings in Queensland.) Seen by many in the industry as a cash grab and even 'rent theft', industry associations such as Property Investment Professionals of Australia (PIPA) and the Real Estate Institute of Queensland (REIQ) campaigned against the controversial legislation. In September 2022, the Queensland Government shelved the changes — which isn't to say they might not emerge again in the future.

Other Costs to Be Aware Of

Owning property incurs a number of costs additional to the inevitable charges of mortgage interest, council rates, body corporate fees and taxes. You need to also budget for utilities, the cost of managing the property (if an investment property) and insurance. And you need to think about the costs of potential improvements — to ensure the property keeps meeting your needs or those of tenants, and to keep its market value growing.

Utility charges

Owner-occupiers need to cover all utility charges that apply for a property — including gas and electricity, water and any phone and internet charges. If you already own a home or even if you're a renter, no doubt you already have a fair idea of what these charges are likely to be at any new home you purchase.

For investors, the past two decades have seen much headway in transferring the costs associated with utility usage to the people responsible for the actual usage — tenants. In the 1990s, state governments began introducing legislation to encourage (or in some cases to make it compulsory) for landlords to install individual meters on most new properties (and some older developments) so that usage of water, electricity and gas could be measured by the individual unit forming part of a block. When that occurred and tenants had to start paying for their own usage instead of landlords paying, usage dropped dramatically.

Usage charges are, therefore, now largely paid by tenants; however, some caveats exist to this, depending on the location of the property. In circumstances where individual meters aren't installed, the landlord is still required to pay for those charges where they can't be separated. Where individual meters are connected, electricity, gas and water usage are charged directly by the utility company to the tenant. In some locations, the property also needs to be water-efficient for usage charges to be transferred to tenants.

The utility cost that's still usually levied to the property owner is non-usage charges for water. The provision of the water service, sewerage service and drainage is still generally levied to the landlord, and these can still be a significant proportion of each bill.

Agents' fees

One of the biggest ongoing fees associated with property investment is the cost of employing an agent. Agents in Australia tend to charge a percentage of the rent to manage your property. What you get for your monthly fee varies enormously, as does the quality of letting or leasing agents.

The base fee charged by agents is usually about 8 per cent of the rent (plus 10 per cent GST). Fees are usually higher for short-term rental properties, such as Airbnb, holiday homes and weekend rentals. For full-time tenanted properties, if your monthly rent is $2,400 (the equivalent of $600 a week), your agent may generally charge you about $211 (including GST) a month to look after your property. Most months, for most properties, all the agent has to do for that fee is ensure that the rent is being paid on time.

The agent is also responsible for chasing up the rent if the tenant forgets to pay or has trouble paying (although the property owner also needs to keep an eye on the agent when things get patchy). When everything is going smoothly, the tenant is paying on time and the property is holding itself together, agents seem to be overpaid. But when something goes wrong, having an agent to organise repairs, deal with tenants and attend court can be the cheapest employment contract you've ever signed.

REMEMBER

Some very good agents out there charge at the lower end of the scale and some very bad ones charge top dollar. Price isn't necessarily any indication of quality. The fees associated with agents are usually tax-deductible.

AGENTS' ECONOMIES OF SCALE

If you're looking to invest in property, you might also be considering managing that property yourself. Although nothing is wrong with opting to manage your own property, we don't recommend you do so, especially if you're a first-time property investor, or you're an investor who owns only one or two properties. Here's why.

The average cost of employing a property manager for an Australian property is a small percentage of the total cost of owning of the property, generally anywhere from $2,000 to $4,000 annually, depending on the property's rent. For that price, you get a professional, or a team, who knows the many laws that govern running properties in your state. Usually, the agent knows what to do, has experience in doing it and has the systems in place to do it quickly. If a problem with a tenant arises, an agent can quickly organise the paperwork to get to the right tribunal to sort the matter, because it's something agents occasionally have to do. If an emergency occurs in the middle of the night or on a long weekend, agents know immediately which tradespeople will take the call. They also know a few strategies when it comes to getting tenants to pay outstanding rent (although they're certainly not perfect in that regard). Think of the time you might spend collecting rent and answering maintenance requests, even if you own only two properties in different parts of your city. Agents also have a good idea of what the local properties are renting for and how much your property is worth. Their fees are a small price to pay for peace of mind.

On the other hand, managing your own properties may make sense if you run a significant portfolio, own a block of apartments or have plenty of available time and the interest to become acquainted with the laws and processes you need to follow.

Property improvements

Properties require regular updating, regardless of whether they're occupied by the owner or rented out. Not every year, but every now and then a property needs to be spruced up. If you want to ensure your property remains in excellent condition as your home and continues to meet your needs, or is attractive to tenants, sometimes you need to splash on a coat of paint, modernise some of the fixtures and fittings, replace carpet and curtains or even give an entire room or two a new feel.

Although you can easily research what each of these items cost, what's important to know for investors is how they're treated in relation to tax. Most of the other ongoing expenses covered in this chapter (including agents' fees, land tax, council rates, body corporate fees, utility charges, gardening and insurance) can be claimed in the same year that the expense occurred. That's not necessarily the case with physical improvements to the home.

Some improvements on investment properties are seen as repairs and maintenance and some categorised as capital improvements. The difference is important, because it determines the speed with which you can claim the item's cost in your tax return. As a broad rule, big items need to be depreciated over many years, whereas small items can be claimed against the investor's income in the year the expense occurred. If you need to replace one venetian blind that costs a few hundred dollars, you may be able to claim that in tax in the year it's purchased (thereby getting a return according to your marginal tax rate). But a new dishwasher will probably have to be depreciated over a number of years.

Insurance

Don't consider starting out in real estate ownership if you aren't prepared to be properly covered with insurance. Property assets are usually very big and expensive assets and having one burn down or devastated by a storm can set you back years (maybe decades) if the house isn't properly insured.

Being a property owner, you'd be foolish to go without various types of insurance. The first and most obvious is house and contents insurance — to ensure the building can be rebuilt if it's wiped out by the aforementioned disasters. Make sure the insurance covers the fixtures and fittings (so you don't end up short of money to carpet the place and put window furnishings in).

For investors, several providers in Australia also offer landlord's insurance. This allows an investor to cover lost rent if the house becomes uninhabitable for various reasons or if you get the tenant from hell. Both house and contents insurance and landlord's insurance are options designed to protect the property itself and are fully tax-deductible for investment properties.

Chapter **7**

Evaluating Property and Making an Offer

The price that you offer for your home or investment property can either improve or explode your chances of being the new owner. That's because if you offer too low, you could offend not only the seller but also the sales agent. If you offer too high, well, you might well get to sign on the dotted line, but your finance might fall over because the bank valuation doesn't marry up with the price that you were prepared to pay. However, doing your research can help to ensure the price you offer gives you the best chance of securing the property at the right price.

You're likely to log many hours locating and assessing potential property purchases — even if you've chosen to work with a team of experts to help you. Then comes the moment when you must decide whether you want to try to buy a property or keep looking for a more attractive opportunity. In this chapter, we discuss how to use your property assessment to determine your top buying price, and how to negotiate a deal that meets your needs as well as considering those of the seller. Next, we briefly cover the all-important details of real estate contracts. Finally, we look at the importance of deciding on ownership structure — before you sign on the dotted line.

Valuation: Working Out How Much to Pay

As mentioned throughout this book, we strongly recommend using an expert team to help you during your property investment journey. Professionals such as buyers' agents, qualified property investment advisers (QPIAs) and valuers can come up with a valuation figure for a potential property that's likely to be far more accurate than your own approach to property pricing and potentially save you a heap of time — and money. But it also helps to understand the three basic methods that valuers use to determine a property's value, so in the following sections we explain these methods.

Usually, each method arrives at a slightly different estimate of value. You or the valuer needs to weigh up which one makes the most sense for the particular property — it won't always be the one that arrives at the lowest value. But lenders require valuations to protect their position — that is, to make sure that if they're suddenly forced to take possession of the property and sell, they're less likely to suffer a loss.

REMEMBER

Property valuation isn't an exact science. Although property valuers apply their skill and experience to determine a precise market value on a property, it is accepted that variances, to some degree, will occur between two different valuers. That said, the variations should not be extreme if both valuers applied the same principals when conducting their assessments.

Market data (sales-comparison) approach

The *market data* (or sales-comparison) approach applies the economic concept of substitution to real estate — essentially, that the value of a given property should be approximately the same as a comparable property that provides similar benefits.

You've probably seen this concept before. You'd expect two similar homes built by the same builder at the same time on comparable lots to sell for analogous prices. (Of course, no two homes are identical, and you inevitably need to adjust for small changes.)

REMEMBER

The accuracy of the market data valuation approach relies on sourcing sufficient recent sales of comparable properties. This approach is primarily used for houses, apartments, units, town-houses and small apartment buildings, because sales are typically more plentiful.

If completed sales are insufficient to arrive at a reasonable valuation, valuers may consider current listings and pending sales, but they usually discount such potential transactions because they're not finalised, and many things can happen before a sale.

Typically, valuers look for at least three comparable properties in close proximity to the subject property. Of course, the usage and type of real estate should be the same or similar — a good comparison should be similar in age, size, amenities and condition of property. How recently the sale occurred is also very important.

Valuers strive to find several comparable properties, but the reality is that every property is unique, so absolutely identical comparable sales or listings are unlikely. So, appraisers need to make either positive or negative adjustments to account for the differences. They factor all of these variances into an adjustment to the price and then calculate an indicated value for the subject property.

For example, say you want to purchase a house to use as your home or to can rent out as an investment property. You see a property listed for $705,000 that's 400 square metres with a three-bedroom, two-bathroom house on it. The property is about ten years old, in good condition and has a great location on a corner lot. Using the sales-comparison method, you want to know the value of this property, so you contact a local agent and gather the recent sales data for comparable houses that have recently sold in the same suburb. Table 7-1 contains the information you've collected for recent sales of houses.

Because the properties are different, you need to make some adjustments to formulate a price for the proposed property. The adjustments are made for features that typical buyers and sellers in that area feel have a material impact on value, either positively or negatively. For example, in many parts of Australia, a property with air conditioning is more desirable than one without, and property condition is important in all markets.

TABLE 7-1 Market Data Summary

Category	Proposed Acquisition	Property A	Property B	Property C
Price	$705,000	$665,000	$700,000	$720,000
Age	10 years	9 years	14 years	New
Location	Corner lot	Mid-block	Corner lot	Mid-block
Condition	Good	Fair	Good	Excellent
Features	Air conditioning	N/A	N/A	Air conditioning
Sale date	On market	10 months ago	Last week	Last month

After researching the local market to establish what factors are important to buyers and sellers, determine what adjustments should be made for the subject property based on its age, location and condition, and the fact that it has air conditioning (see Table 7-2):

>> **Property A** is comparable in age to the subject property but is clearly inferior — it doesn't have air conditioning or the corner lot and is only in fair condition. The property sold 10 months ago, and your research shows that prices for comparable properties in the suburb have risen 3 to 4 per cent since then. You make adjustments for the corner lot ($10,000), condition ($10,000), air conditioning ($5,000) and market timing ($15,000). So, overall, you expect that, if this property was on a corner lot, was sold today in good condition and had air conditioning, it would've sold for approximately $40,000 more than the actual sale ten months ago, or an adjusted sale price of $705,000, to bring the property in line for comparison with the subject property.

>> **Property B** is a little older but, because it's been well maintained and is in good condition, no adjustment is necessary for that factor. The property is on a corner lot and also sold just last week, so no adjustments are necessary for these factors. However, it doesn't have air conditioning ($5,000). With air conditioning, this property would've likely sold for $705,000.

>> **Property C** is brand new, has air conditioning and sold only last month. The only disadvantage when compared with your proposed investment is this property's location in the middle of the block. Overall, your research indicates that the price difference for brand-new properties is $15,000 higher than a ten-year-old property like the subject property. But comparable properties located in the middle of the block sell for $5,000 less. (**Note:** While a corner block may add $10,000 to the price, being in the middle doesn't automatically take off $10,000. The amount depends on other factors in the block's position.) Therefore, you need to adjust the Property C price lower by $15,000 for age and higher by $5,000 for the inferior location, which is a net downward adjustment of $10,000 and leads you to an adjusted value of $710,000.

In reviewing the results of your analysis and adjustments in Table 7-2, you feel that the asking price is right in line with (if not slightly below) the current market price for comparable properties in the neighbourhood. You decide that, if you can purchase the property for $705,000 or less, you'll have a good investment.

TABLE 7-2 **Adjusting Sales Price to Determine Value**

	Proposed Property	Property A	Property B	Property C
Price	$705,000	$665,000	$700,000	$720,000
Adjustment	0	$40,000	$5,000	($10,000)
Value	$705,000	$705,000	$705,000	$710,000

Cost approach

The cost approach to real estate valuation also relies on the concept of substitution, whereby an informed buyer wouldn't pay more for a property than the cost of building a comparable property. This approach to real estate valuation can be used when data on comparable sales is unavailable, but it's more commonly used — and even the preferred method — for proposed construction or brand-new properties.

REMEMBER

The replacement cost of a property often can be an indicator of *barriers to entry* that exist in the market. Barriers to entry in an area can include shortage of buildable land, strong anti-apartment sentiments or vocal community groups with environmental concerns.

Owning real estate in high demand with high barriers to entry for competing properties is one of the best ways to ensure the success of your real estate investments.

In determining valuation using the cost approach, the property is divided between the land and improvements (buildings) and each segment is valued separately. Here are the steps a valuer may follow in applying the cost approach:

1. **Estimate the value of the land if vacant and being used in its highest and best use.**

   The valuer looks for sales of comparable vacant land in the area.

2. **Estimate the current cost to reproduce the existing building as new, before depreciation.**

3. **Estimate all forms of accrued depreciation and deduct that amount from the calculation in Step 2 to arrive at the approximate cost to reproduce the building in its current condition.**

4. **Combine the value of the land and the value of the depreciated improvements to arrive at the total value of the property.**

Accrued depreciation can be caused by three factors:

>> **Physical deterioration:** Normal wear and tear that occurs from use over time, such as a 12-year-old roof that can normally be expected to last 20 years.

>> **Functional obsolescence:** Decline in the usefulness of a property due to changes in preferences by consumers — for example, a home with three bedrooms and only one bathroom.

>> **External obsolescence:** Loss in value resulting from external forces, such as the major employer in town closing down, with longer travel times to comparable jobs.

Using the house example from the previous section, you determine that the cost of a comparable vacant lot would be $430,000. Checking with local builders in your market indicates that the cost to build a new house would be $2,200 per square metre; however, because the building is ten years old, some wear and tear is inevitable. You, therefore, estimate that the cost to rebuild the property in its current condition is $1,950 per square metre (it isn't an exact science). The property is 140 square metres, so the total value of the depreciated improvements is $273,000.

Adding the land value of $430,000 to the $273,000 value for the depreciated improvements gives an overall value of the property of $703,000 using the cost method of valuation.

Calculating a yield-based return

If looking for a property as an investment, an important tool when deciding on which property to purchase can be the income return of a subject property, in relation to other properties in the area. Determining the yield of a property can be a far more important source of information for an investor, particularly first-time investors, or investors in their early years of ownership.

The yield of a property is the annual income return that the property is promising, which can help determine whether you can afford the property or not.

The yield of a property is calculated by finding out what the weekly or monthly rent of the property is (or is expected to be, which you may be able to find out via local real estate agents), annualising that figure and then dividing it by the property's purchase price. This then allows you to compare it to other similar properties available on the market at a given time.

TIP

When annualising a rent figure, don't just multiply the weekly or monthly rent by 52 weeks or 12 months. As a property investor, you have to plan for the fact that your property is likely to spend some time vacant. More often than not, renters are short-term tenants who may only rent the property for one year or two. So, the property is likely to go through times of vacancy between when old tenants move out and new tenants can be found. To be conservative, you should probably allow for your property to be vacant for certain periods each year — in metropolitan areas, factor in at least two weeks of vacancy in a year and allow for perhaps three to four weeks a year in non-metropolitan areas. So, when you get a tenant that stays for five years, you have a rare tenant indeed — five years with a fully leased property is wonderfully consistent cash flow. Hold on to those tenants.

Allowing for average vacancy rates, the annual rental of a property that rents for $600 a week is, therefore, $30,000 — $600 × 50 weeks (rather than 52 weeks). If you're likely to pay $660,000 for the property, the annual yield is $40,000/$660,000, which is 4.5 per cent. If the property is only being leased for $570 a week, the yield is $28,500/$660,000, or 4.31 per cent.

This reasonably simple calculation allows you to compare one property to the next, if you can get reasonable estimates on what the property might sell and lease for.

REMEMBER

Annualising your rent figure gives you your gross yield. You have plenty of costs, which can often suck up all of that yield and more. But finding out the gross yield percentage is important for first-time investors, because lower yielding properties generally mean that you have to find more money from your own pocket to support the property until rents rise.

All some investors want from a property is yield, or income. They may be at a stage of their life where they don't feel they need capital growth anymore, but do need income from the property to support their retirement or to reduce their working hours. That's completely understandable.

WARNING

High yields aren't everything. Higher yielding properties can have their own drawbacks, or be typical of certain styles of properties (flats, for instance) that may not produce the capital gain that you seek from your property. Although higher yields mean the less money you have to find from other sources on a monthly basis, yield isn't everything.

Understand that yield and growth — in all investments, not just property — are a trade-off. A very general rule is that the highest yielding investments tend to be the lowest growth. It's not a hard and fast rule, but it's an important rule that also applies to property investment.

Finding properties where you can add value

For investors, finding properties that are offering a lower yield or rental return can be profitable. You want to buy an investment property when you determine that the property has a strong likelihood of producing future increases in rent or better capital growth. So, you should look for properties where your analysis shows that the income for the property can be increased simply and cheaply.

However, certain clues when putting your value on a property can indicate whether a property really has rents that are below market. Properties that are constantly occupied with little vacancy time are prime candidates. Other telltale signs are properties that have low turnover and then have multiple applicants for those rare vacancies. Economics 101 says that, if demand exceeds supply, the price is too low.

TIP

A common question asked is, 'How do I find underpriced properties?' Our experience indicates you're more likely to find characteristics of underpricing of investment properties (such as below-market rents) with owners who are older, have no mortgage and typically have exhausted the advantages of depreciation deductions on their tax return.

Look for properties where you can increase value over the first few years of ownership. These value-added properties are those that allow you to increase rents with comparatively little effort or expense — such as a new paint job or installing an air conditioner. As we point out in the preceding section, the value of a property increases with an increase in rent.

Negotiating Basics

Regardless of whether you're purchasing a home or an investment property, an important concept to grasp is this: You make money in property when you buy. If you purchase a well-located and physically sound property below market value and replacement cost, the property can provide you with excellent growth and returns (if you're an investor) for many years. Superior knowledge combined with superior negotiating leads to superior returns. The following sections explain how to be a champion negotiator.

Selecting negotiating styles

A lot of forces are at work — and a lot of vested interests — when it comes to the negotiation of a final sales price of a given property. The buyer is seeking the lowest price to minimise their mortgage and, potentially, maximise future returns. Vendors want the highest price to maximise the return they're about to crystallise. And the agent . . . well, in reality, the agent doesn't care what price it sells for, as long as it sells! The way that properties are usually sold means that agents are primarily remunerated only if they make a sale. Of secondary concern to an agent is the actual sales price — although the best agents always aim to achieve the best results for their selling clients.

CONDITIONING VENDOR EXPECTATIONS

WARNING

When it comes to dodgy selling practices, 'conditioning' tops the list, as far as we're concerned. Conditioning is a process whereby agents tell a prospective vendor that they believe the property can achieve a certain price (say, $550,000). Then, close to the auction, or as offers start coming in, the agent tries to get the vendor to lower her expectations for a sales price (to, say, $520,000). This is done to ensure that a sale occurs, because most agents don't get paid unless an actual sale of the property takes place. Some agents quote high to win the business from the vendor in the first place, and then try to cut the vendor's expectations — and it happens particularly regularly in markets with little price growth or few sales occurring.

Nicola had the experience of selling one of her properties in 2021 with the sales agent using every known tactic in his playbook in an attempt to condition me to take a lower sales price. Unfortunately for him, she used to be responsible for running sales success conferences when she was the head of corporate affairs at the Real Estate Institute of Queensland (REIQ), so had heard it all before. The agent tried very hard to get Nicola to accept $499,000 for her property — when she had been very clear from the outset that she would not sell it for less than $550,000. In fact, Nicola told him she would just withdraw it from sale and put it back on the rental market if she didn't achieve this figure. The hard pressure tactics from the agent continued for the next week, to no avail.

When the agent, clearly quite frustrated that his techniques weren't working on Nicola, managed to extract an offer of $540,000 from a buyer, she negotiated to pay him less commission if she accepted the deal. It seems Nicola may have been the better negotiator than the agent appointed to act on her behalf!

Some people argue that ethics and morals have a place in purchasing property. We certainly don't condone shonky business practices (and you need to watch out for some agent practices that are, in fact, illegal), but morals and ethics mean different things to different people. Sometimes you'll do better out of a transaction as a buyer than the seller did. That's your aim as a property buyer — to get property for prices below the market value. But, even when the buyer believes she got a steal, the vendor could still be ecstatic with the price she received in return. Surely, you'd think, only one of them is right. Sometimes, they're both understandably happy with the final price.

Along with conditioning (see the nearby sidebar), another potential concern for vendors is when offers come from parties related to the selling agent. An agent who introduces a buyer who is a personal friend has a clear conflict of interest. While it's obviously okay for homebuyers and investors to develop working relationships with agents, it's a morally murky area if the agent helps a friend to buy a property off one of his clients when it's possible that the agent may not be working to get the client the highest price possible.

The fuzzy concept of morals in purchasing property is difficult to reconcile with the intent of property as an investment asset, which is to make money. The old saying that 'you make your money when you buy' means that buying a property below market price — and the lower the better — gives you more money when you sell. If a vendor isn't properly informed, who's to blame? Certainly not the potential buyer!

REMEMBER

In all fields of purchasing and investment, information is queen. If one player has superior knowledge to another player, she has an advantage. Those who do the most research are in the best position to profit.

Desperate vendors, uneducated vendors and foolish vendors are always going to be around. And some vendors really don't know enough to be playing in a particular market. But those who refuse to seek proper advice from trustworthy professionals have only themselves to blame.

Although it's true that real estate agents are a close-knit community of professionals who network — and getting on the wrong side of agents in an area that you're looking to buy in can hamper your success — they're also salespeople with a product to sell, the price of which is (usually) negotiable. Being a bit hard-nosed, without agents finding your demeanour offensive, is almost expected. In fact, not having a bit of toughness about your offers leaves you, as the buyer, open to being manipulated.

Here are some of the necessary negotiating tactics that show strength, without being off-putting:

>> **Setting a time limit:** If you're making an offer in a private sale, particularly in a weak market with few buyers and many potential sellers, put a sunset clause on your offer. It's not quite the 'my way or the highway' style, but it puts a little pressure back on the vendor (whose agents are expert at putting pressure on buyers). If you've made a reasonable offer that's at about the market price, even if a little on the low side, give the vendor 24 or 48 hours. If you make your offer on a Thursday, give the vendor until close-of-business Friday. Don't let the vendor have the weekend, giving her another 48 hours to canvas more offers.

>> **Lowballing:** If a house has been on the market for a long time in any market, you never know just how desperate vendors have become. They may have knocked back a reasonable offer a month ago in the belief that someone would offer more soon. But, if no further offers were forthcoming, they may now be getting desperate. Talk to the agent. Find out what offers have been rejected before, but be careful to not submit an offensive lowball offer.

>> **Keeping your cards close to your chest:** Don't tell the agent financial details that she doesn't need to know, or that could be used against you. Agents don't need to know what your budget is — knowing your upper limit for a purchase could certainly be used against you. The correct answer to questions about the size of your wallet is, 'It depends on the property.' But being rude to agents is unnecessary, and allowing them to show you properties that are definitely out of your price range is a waste of your time and theirs.

TIP

While a property remains unsold, its agents are still waiting to receive their commission. Getting them onside with a property they are sick of the sight of — perhaps because the vendor knocked back reasonable offers or because one too many bids have fallen through — may even get them to become your ally in trying to get a below-market sale through.

WARNING

The problem with many aggressive negotiating techniques is that you can get so wrapped up in just 'making the deal' that you forget what you're doing. You can make some serious mistakes and buy properties you should've eliminated during your pre-offer due diligence. Don't get emotionally involved in any potential property — or negotiation process.

Building your knowledge base

The most important negotiating tool in a property purchase is superior knowledge. You need to know more about your proposed property acquisition than anyone else, especially the seller. You need to know about the property, nearby properties and the economic data that could point to this property being in the path of progress. (Although more important for investors, this is also good information for homebuyers to be aware of.) For investors, knowledge of local and state laws is often helpful as well.

REMEMBER

Regardless of whether you're buying a home or an investment, you need to set a maximum price you can pay for a property. If investing, you're also looking to receive a solid return on your investment in light of the associated risks.

Do your homework

We don't suggest that you mislead anyone, but it's amazing how many current owners of property just don't pay attention to even the most basic publicly available information. Your research with the local council may give you the vision to upgrade and renovate a property to achieve its full potential (and value) because you've discovered that a major new employer is moving into the area. For home owners, this new employer may lead to an increase in overall amenities and services in the areas. For investors, it may mean demand is highly likely to dramatically increase for half-vacant and tired commercial properties or properties to house incoming executives — like the one you're considering for purchase.

With property buying and investing, you're likely to be more successful in negotiating great real estate deals if you not only have a good real estate investment team, but also know the important factors that affect supply and demand in the local market.

Maybe you're seeing local companies growing rapidly and hiring lots of new workers. You know that, because of a local housing shortage, many new families moving into the area will be unable to afford a new home and will need to rent instead. That's a good sign that rents will increase, and the demand will be high for nice three- or four-bedroom rental houses located in quiet cul-de-sacs near good schools. These new families will need additional services, facilities and shops — and this can only be a good thing for all home owners in the area. Clearly, you can use this information to properly negotiate the purchase of prime homes in such a market.

The reason that negotiating is so important to being successful with your real estate purchases and investments is this: You want to pay the seller only for the current value of the property as-is and not the future potential that your skill and expertise will create. Patience, vision and perseverance are also great virtues when it comes to making the best real estate deals. If you're unwilling to do the homework necessary to justify the right price, you're more likely to overpay for real estate. Although an occasional seller dramatically underestimates the true market value of a property, the vast majority of properties you see offered for sale are overpriced — often because of the current owner's emotional attachment to their home.

Determine the current supply and demand in the marketplace so you know whether it's a buyer's or seller's market. You can still make some great purchases and investments, but you need to be realistic. Buying in a seller's market at prices above replacement cost is dangerous.

REMEMBER

As the potential purchaser, discover as much as you can about the property (and the owner) before making an offer. How long has the property been on the market? What are its flaws? Why is the owner selling? The more you know about the property you want to buy and about the seller's motivations, the better your ability to make an acceptable offer.

Figure out the seller's motivations

Some agents love to talk and will tell you the life history of the seller. Encourage this free flow of information. The goal for you is to get the agent to reveal helpful information (without you sharing too much pertinent information about yourself). Always seek the answer to the most important question: 'Why is the vendor selling?' The answer can tell you a lot about the seller's motivation and may give you a reason to either move on or be calm and patient with your negotiations.

GET-RICH-QUICK SPRUIKERS' STRATEGIES DON'T PAN OUT

We hate to be the bearers of bad news, but all of those get-rich-quick property spruikers don't tell the full story when they and their testimonials say how easy it was for them to start with nothing and suddenly own vast real estate holdings that all seem magically to be worth millions and provide great cash flow. If it were really that easy, the gurus wouldn't be telling you about it — they'd be busy making great deals just for themselves.

There *are* times when you buy just before the market takes off and you can't lose. But the worst spruikers, when it comes to giving unrealistic expectations to potential property owners, are usually just the best salespeople.

The old adage 'If it sounds too good to be true, it is too good to be true' applies to real estate — and particularly the thought that the best real estate is available to the average person at unbelievably favourable terms. So much capital is available to owners of real estate that even truly desperate sellers usually have the ability to borrow more money. The interest rates and terms may be horrendous, but money is almost always available for any property that isn't a toxic waste dump — an owner doesn't need to give a property away unless it has no equity. Remember, there's no such thing as a free lunch — you usually get what you pay for.

The most frightening pitches for real estate have been made by spruikers trying to flog property in the 'next big place' that will cash in on a seemingly history-making industry boom in usually small regional locations. Pitches involving a small town where 'a large mining company is about to get approval for a mine that will last for 25 years' have become an all-too-easy way for developers to flog off properties in remote locations, claiming that the mine sites will need dozens, if not hundreds, of houses to satisfy the needs of mine workers. History shows us that many unwary investors who bought into this hype have ended up with properties not worth what they paid for them, as well as ones that they often can't even rent out.

Be *extremely* wary of buying properties promoted as sure things. In far too many cases, people have signed on the dotted line . . . and then

(continued)

(continued)

found out that the mine has not been approved or would never have been approved, or the company has changed its mind because the project is no longer viable — and they are left with a worthless investment. Also make sure you are working with bona fide experts, especially when it comes to property investment advice, instead of blindly following the sales pitch of people who are just trying to line their own pockets.

Also, if you know enough about the seller's motivation, you can avoid wasting your time negotiating with someone who isn't really motivated to sell. Some vendors are really just testing the market or are willing to sell only if they can get a price well over the market value.

Figure out how to spot these fake vendors early on. Look for the warning signs, such as unexplained delays in responding to offers or questions, a reluctance to answer questions or give you access to the property, and an uncooperative attitude across the board. If you see these signs, you don't even want to make an offer on the property.

REMEMBER

We can't say this often enough: Don't give out any information about your motivations that give the seller added negotiating leverage. The less you say about how much you like the property or your reasons for making the offer, the better. For example, many vendors are able to stick to their full-price terms and as-is condition of the property if they know the buyer has a big enough budget at her disposal or has tight time restrictions. A buyer wanting to wrap up a sale before heading back home interstate may suddenly be agreeable to many reasonable conditions requested by a seller.

Bring your data to the table

Bring facts that back up your argument to the bargaining table. Collect comparable sales data to support your price. Too often, homebuyers and investors pick a number out of the air when they make an offer. If you were the seller, would you be persuaded to lower your asking price? Pointing to recent and comparable property sales to justify your offer strengthens your case. Sellers often don't select properly comparable properties — preferring to creatively use just those prior sales that provide for the highest possible asking price. The heart of negotiating is information.

WARNING

If the property needs repairs, never rely on quotes provided by the seller. You must independently verify the numbers with licensed contractors. You can also use these written quotes to support your position regarding the true cost to make needed repairs rather than just making verbal representations that a prudent buyer would treat sceptically. However, you should always leave yourself wriggle room. Remember that even with the most comprehensive quotes from the top industry professionals, any significant renovation or remodelling project is likely to take longer and cost more than is estimated.

Assembling attractive and realistic offers

Since we don't want to just tell you what not to do, here are some examples of realistic and creative ways to negotiate and structure a real estate offer that accurately reflects the value of the property and, if investing, also provides you with a reasonable return.

Factoring in fix-up costs

Say you come across an opportunity to buy a great three-bedroom, two-bathroom house. You've spent some time investigating and you know the area is terrific. (If looking for a home, perhaps you already live in the area.) The house would be an ideal home for your growing family or, if investing, a great rental because it's two blocks from a new school. You estimate that the property will rent for $2,750 per month, and the market indicates strong demand for rental homes. The seller is asking $730,000, which appears to be its market value — based on the home seeming to have no deferred maintenance. But, remember — all rental properties have some deferred maintenance, so you call your home-inspection contractor. Her report indicates that, overall, the property is in decent condition and the big-ticket items of appliances and flooring have recently been replaced. But she also has some bad news: The roof needs to be replaced in the next few years. You contact three reputable roofing contractors, and the best value quote for a roof replacement that'll last 20 years is $25,000. You also estimate that you'll need about $8,000 in minor repairs and upgrades to the landscaping and the irrigation system.

What should you pay? If you said $697,000, you aren't necessarily wrong, but you're not providing any room for contingencies — or any compensation or reimbursement for your time and the risk involved in overseeing and coordinating this work. We suggest you take your actual conservative estimates for all repairs and add at least 50 per cent. Cover those surprises that are likely to occur and compensate yourself for the time, effort and risk associated with renovations. Contractors and other professionals always allow for contingencies, overheads and profit when they present their quotes, so why should you — as a home owner or real estate investor who invests your efforts using your own DIY or contracting skills — not be equally compensated? This mistake is one of the biggest that novice real estate homebuyers and investors make — and can avoid.

Creatively meeting the seller's price

Price is only one of several negotiable items, but it's the first clause the seller reviews in a purchase offer. Because many sellers are fixated on the price they'll receive for the property (perhaps they're set on beating what the Joneses got last year for their house a few doors down), you can offer the full price, but seek other concessions in order to reduce the effective cost of buying the property.

One way to reduce the cost is to get the seller to pay for certain repairs or improvements. The buyer should consider asking the seller to correct all health and safety items before settlement. But other items can also be negotiated. For example, rather than have the seller patch that 30-year-old roof that you'll be replacing anyway, ask to take the cost of the repairs off the purchase price. This is obviously easier to request in a buyer's market, when sellers don't have numerous offers on the table. In a seller's market, where the seller is entertaining multiple offers, they may stop discussions with you if you make the negotiations too difficult.

TIP

The time that you need to settle on your purchase is also a bargaining chip. Some sellers need cash soon and may concede other points if you can settle quickly — in, say, 30 days instead of 60, or 60 days instead of 90.

Finally, don't fall in love with a property — especially as an investor but also if you're looking for your next home. Keep searching for other properties even when you make an offer — you may be negotiating with an unmotivated vendor.

Making Your Offer

The purchase and sale of real estate is always done in writing. The most critical document in any transaction is the purchase agreement, which is usually referred to as the *contract of sale*. After you've found a property that meets your buying or investment goals, you need to pick up the seller's contract and get your solicitor or conveyancer to look over the contract for irregularities prior to making your offer.

Understanding the basics of contracts

A real estate contract is a legally binding written agreement between two or more persons regarding an exchange of some sort. These contracts are legally enforceable sets of promises that must be performed and that rely on the basics of contract law.

A legally binding contract must include consideration (usually money) passing between the parties, an intention from all parties to be bound to the contract, a meeting of the minds of the parties as to the contents of the contract and an element of clarity so the terms of the contract may be interpreted, understood and enforced by a court, if necessary. Such a contract is valid because it contains all of the necessary elements that make it legally enforceable. In the following list, we outline the basic elements of a legally binding and enforceable real estate contract. The terms may sound a bit technical, but you need to be familiar with them:

>> **Legally competent parties:** Every party to the transaction must have legal capacity, which is defined as being of legal age (usually 18 in Australia) and having the mental capacity to understand the consequences of their actions. Convicted criminals and certain mentally ill persons may not have legal capacity. Be careful when dealing with older persons if they seem to have any difficulty understanding or communicating. Politely enquire if they have anyone who is acting on their behalf in a representative capacity.

>> **An offer:** An offer to purchase property is a written communication to the owner of the buyer's willingness to purchase the property on the terms indicated. Unless an expiration clause is included, the seller may accept an offer at any time before it's rescinded by the buyer.

Most offers should have a specific expiration time. ('This offer is valid until Friday, 19 June, at 5 pm AEST only.') Back up that time limit to prevent the seller from using the offer as a negotiating tool with other interested parties, shopping your offer around, trying to entice other buyers to raise their offer. Also, if the offer is open-ended, the buyer has to actively withdraw the offer, which is more work and trouble than simply having the offer expire after some passage of time.

» **Acceptance:** Acceptance is a positive written response in a timely manner to the exact terms of an offer. A legal requirement to have acceptance is that the buyer must be given legal notice of the acceptance. Often, the seller won't accept the offer as presented, but will propose changes in the terms or conditions — which is a counteroffer.

» **Counteroffer:** Legally a new offer, where the original offer is rejected and is void. Counteroffers can go back and forth until both buyer and seller have agreed and the final accepted offer becomes the binding agreement between the parties. Just like offers, counteroffers should be in writing and can also be rescinded at any time prior to acceptance.

» **Consideration:** Payment of money or something of value, which is typically offered by the buyer to the seller in exchange for the seller entering into the contract for purchase of real estate. A real estate contract isn't binding if each party doesn't offer at least some consideration to the other party.

» **Clearly and uniquely identified property:** A requirement so no uncertainty exists about precisely which property is being sold and transferred to the buyer. Typically, a legal description of the property is used.

» **Legal purpose:** The real estate contract must be for a legal purpose and can't be for an illegal act. An example of a potential transaction in which a buyer would want to cancel the purchase is if she is purchasing a house with the intent to run her company there but discovers during the settlement process that such use violates local prohibitions against operating a business in a residentially zoned area.

» **Written contract:** A written contract is required for all enforceable transfers of real estate. All terms and conditions of the purchase agreement or sales contract must be set out in writing, even for minor items that may seem inconsequential. The written contract helps ensure no confusion exists about what's included in the sale. For example, if you want to make sure that the supplies in the maintenance shop for a commercial or apartment building are included and not taken before the sale, you must specify it in the contract. Remember that if something isn't in writing, you're unlikely to prevail.

WARNING

Agreements for the sale of real estate must be in writing or they're unenforceable. Never make an oral agreement of any type regarding real estate, no matter how convenient, expedient or reasonable it may seem at the time. Have your solicitor or conveyancer read all contracts of sale before you sign.

Besides all the legal elements, real estate sales contracts specify the sale price and the terms and conditions (see the section 'Using conditions effectively', later in this chapter).

Completing the contract of sale

The contract of sale (some states may have different names for the contract itself) is the legal document that outlines the details of the transaction for your proposed purchase of the property.

WARNING

Victorian real estate agents also have a document known as a *contract note* — described in some quarters as little more than a way for agents to get around the contract of sale itself (in Victoria known as a 'Vendor's Statement' or a 'Section 32') — which may include sale conditions. If you have conditions on the sale written into the contract, the contract note may nullify those conditions. Never sign a contract note without getting the okay from your legal rep, after she has had a chance to read the actual contract of sale. The contract note becomes binding on its own.

WARNING

Always include in the contract note, if one is offered to you, any conditions you want on the sale — no matter what the seller's agent says — before you sign it. If you want the sale to be dependent on acceptable finance or satisfactory building reports, put it in writing on the contract note itself.

No matter what it's called, the sales contract is the most important document in the sale of real estate. It indicates how much you pay, when you pay, the terms and conditions that must be met to close the transaction, and the conditions under which the agreement can be cancelled and the buyer's deposit returned. It starts out with the basics of the names of the sellers and buyers, a description of the property and the proposed financing terms.

Get your solicitor to go over the form in detail and carefully consider the terms that you'll offer in each paragraph (if that's appropriate). Don't leave any blank spaces and have your solicitor mark through any clauses you feel aren't appropriate. Just because a certain clause is pre-printed doesn't mean that you can't cross it out or modify the language to suit your needs. Just make sure that you clearly initial any changes you make and require the other party to also initial every single change and the bottom of each page to ensure that you've agreed on the specific terms.

Some terms are at your discretion, but your solicitor can advise you as to the local practice concerning issues such as the standard for deposits or the length of settlement periods. Your solicitor, in conjunction with the seller's solicitor, can also inform you about local standards for settlement costs.

The remainder of this section covers other key provisions you need to carefully evaluate, because you'll be making many decisions about your offer before the purchase agreement is ready for your signature.

Paying the deposit

The standard deposit paid on signing a real estate contract in Australia used to be 10 per cent, but it really can be whatever figure you can get away with and is usually negotiable. Some savvy homebuyers and property investors like to use a deposit as small as possible, to protect their own cash, or perhaps even a deposit that reflects the selling agent's likely commission — and no more. Your deposit is held in trust by the seller's agent and is usually paid by direct deposit into the trust account.

WARNING

Another way to pay the deposit is through a deposit bond (which is not always accepted by sellers). A deposit bond is a note usually issued through an insurer who promises to pay the deposit at settlement. The cost of a deposit bond — which rose to prominence during the property booms in Victoria and New South Wales in the early 2000s — can often be less than the cost of interest (particularly for longer settlements), but they're often mistrusted, or not accepted, by sellers or developers if buying off-the-plan.

Setting the settlement date

An important term of your purchase offer is the proposed settlement date. The length of the settlement period is a matter of negotiation between the buyer and seller, with consideration given to the length of time needed to complete the sale. Settlements can be any length of time, but are typically requested by sellers at 30, 60 or 90 days. Longer is okay, if it's agreeable to both parties.

Sellers are often interested in closing the property as soon as possible but, in most transactions, particularly where the premises are being occupied by the seller, the actual date depends on a number of factors, including the completion of other property transactions. Investment property buyers usually want longer periods to allow some flexibility in case something goes wrong with financing. Homebuyers may have less flexibility, depending on the settlement or lease end date for the property they're moving out of. All buyers may also occasionally want the right to close the transaction earlier if they've completed their work.

Ultimately, the terms you agree on in the purchase agreement are legally binding. In some cases, the settlement date is really just an estimated date, as a close of sale can involve many moving parts. But the date should be met unless both parties agree to an extension via a written addendum (see 'Ironing out other issues', later in this chapter).

Using conditions effectively

A *condition* in a real estate purchase agreement is simply a contingency that must be fulfilled or an event that may or may not happen before a contract becomes firm and binding. Conditions can be for the benefit of either the seller or the buyer. The seller of an estate property, for example, may put a condition that a court grants probate — the legal registering or acceptance of a deceased person's last will — before the sale is approved. Buyers often have conditions for financing, physical inspections, building and pest inspections, and other items.

Conditions are escape clauses that can protect buyers from purchasing a property that doesn't meet their needs. Purchasing properties without conditions can be extremely risky. Without conditions, buyers would need to be sure, before making an offer, that they have all of the financing in place, that the property is in an acceptable condition and meets their needs, and that the terms are acceptable. Buyers may be unwilling to meet these requirements prior to having some sort of agreement on price in a contract, or they'd discount their offer to account for the additional risk of buying a property without some protection of conditions.

WARNING

Don't forget that you can't set conditions if you buy a property at auction. Auctions are final and, therefore, require buyers to have completed all their due diligence before attending and making a bid. Due diligence includes building and pest inspections, securing financing and any other conditions you may normally consider putting on a property bought through private treaty.

Conditions can allow a prospective buyer the exclusive opportunity to buy the property during a limited time frame but not obligate her to complete the transaction if any issues arise that can't be satisfactorily resolved within the time limits. Naturally, sellers attempt to eliminate unreasonable conditions.

The terms of most sales contracts provide that, by certain defined dates, all of the conditions must be resolved one way or another by the party who stands to gain from the condition. Once in place, a condition can have one of three outcomes:

>> **Conditions can be satisfied.** When conditions are met, the pending sale is no longer subject to cancellation or modification for that particular item. For example, the buyer could comply with the financing contingency upon receiving a written loan commitment at acceptable terms.

>> **The beneficiary of the condition can unilaterally agree to waive or remove the contingency.** For example, the seller may have asked for the sale to be conditional on the timing of the settlement of an unrelated property transaction, but no longer needs that condition to be met.

>> **A condition can be rejected or fail.** The beneficiary of the condition is then no longer obligated to perform under the contract. For example, buyers who have made the sale conditional on a satisfactory pest report may receive a termite-inspection report indicating extensive damage and infestation and then decide that they are no longer

interested in completing the purchase. Under this scenario, the buyers typically receive the return of their deposit — and are glad that they diligently conducted a physical inspection.

TIP

Although the list will vary depending on the property type, size and location, following are condition clauses that we recommend you consider:

>> **Financing:** When buying, be as vague as possible with finance conditions. Use a term similar to 'subject to suitable financing with XYZ Bank', for example, unless the seller insists on you outlining what suitable financing means. In this case, outline the specific terms (type of loan and maximum acceptable interest rate) of a new loan that you require in order to complete the purchase.

>> **Valuation:** This condition demands that an independent valuer of the property arrives at a value equal to or greater than the proposed purchase price. This valuation could be a function of the financing or simply because you don't want to overpay for the property.

>> **Physical inspection:** Some contracts for a property sold through private sale treaty include an inspection clause that mandates that the buyer has access to the property for a certain amount of time to inspect its interior and exterior. Engage a qualified building inspector and, for larger purchases, include specialists in key areas such as roofing, plumbing and electrical systems to conduct a thorough inspection of the entire property. The results of the inspection can be used to negotiate with the seller by giving them the opportunity to make the necessary repairs, adjust the purchase price or simply terminate the purchase agreement.

Ironing out other issues

You also need to be sure that your purchase agreement clearly indicates what chattels are included. Chattels can be a significant factor in all property, but especially apartment buildings because they can include the appliances and window coverings, plus common-area furnishings and fixtures.

Particularly for larger residential and commercial properties, and depending on your plans for the property, you may want the property conveyed with or without tenants. If you are investing and the tenants aren't on valid and enforceable long-term leases, and the property value can be increased by renovation and gaining new tenants, require the seller to deliver the property vacant. (Of course, the tenants will need to move out if you're buying the property as your next home.)

Determining How to Hold Title

One last thing you need to consider before you sign on the dotted line relates to ownership: Who, or what, is going to own the title to the property?

This question might sound silly, with 'I will!' being the possibly all-too-obvious answer. But, although holding the property yourself may be the right option, putting it in your own name may be a costly mistake that could haunt you from day one, or come back to bite you on the backside in years to come, especially if the property is an investment.

WARNING

Making sure you get the property's ownership right before you sign the sale contract is incredibly important from a tax perspective for investors. The wrong ownership structure may see you unnecessarily paying too much tax, while the right structure for the right property may reduce your tax liabilities (in the case of income) or reduce them substantially (in the case of capital gains). And trying to change the ownership after purchase can be costly and involve paying further taxes and duties.

TIP

If you and your partner (if that's applicable) are looking to build a portfolio of many properties over time, consider placing the properties in differing titles (that is, some in one person's name, some in the other person's name and perhaps some in joint names). If you need to sell a property later on to either raise cash or reduce debt, you're then able to choose which property to sell in order to maximise the cash you raise, or minimise the capital gains tax paid, based on each individual's circumstances at the time you need to sell.

No single right answer exists as to the question of how to hold title, because each real estate homebuyer and investor has different perspectives and needs. The legal forms of ownership vary from state to state, so check your options with your solicitor and/or accountant before you sign.

In the following sections, we review some of the basics of each form of ownership — including taxation considerations for investors — so you can build a working understanding of the pros and cons of each of the main alternatives available.

Sole ownership

Being a sole owner is certainly the easiest and cheapest form of ownership and requires no special prerequisites. Simply have title to the property vested in the name of an individual person on the deed and you have a sole proprietor. Owning a property in one name saves on not having to pay the ongoing cost of more complicated ownership structures, such as accounting and legal fees.

Other advantages include

>> **Exclusive rights of ownership:** You have sole discretion over the use of the property, and the right to sell, bequeath or encumber the property any way you see fit.

>> **Simple record keeping:** Be grateful for the simplicity of financial records as a sole owner, but you still need to be disciplined.

REMEMBER

For those individuals in a committed relationship, two obvious options for 'sole ownership' are available in a household — either person could hold the title individually (we deal with joint ownership next). Depending on your individual circumstances, holding the property in only one of your names may make sense. For investors, if one person isn't working or is in a much lower tax bracket than the other, consider placing ownership of positively geared investment real estate in that person's name. A negatively geared property, on the other hand, may be better in the hands of the higher income earner, because the tax deductions create a larger return, which then aids cash flow.

Here's an example of how income tax brackets affect returns for investors: Assume a property with rent of $30,000 has expenses (including interest, insurance, agents' fees and depreciation) of $42,000. The property is negatively geared to the tune of $12,000. Taking into account Australia's tiered marginal tax rate (MTR) structure for incomes at the time of writing, the following shows the impact that income tax has on the returns made by a property that is negatively geared by $12,000:

>> **MTR of 45 per cent:** The investor gets a tax return of $5,400, reducing the net loss to $6,600.

>> **MTR of 37 per cent:** The investor gets a tax return of $4,400, reducing the net loss to $7,560.

>> **MTR 32.5 per cent:** The investor gets a tax return of $3,900, reducing the net loss to $8,100.

>> **MTR 19 per cent:** The investor gets a tax return of $2,280, reducing the net loss to $9,720.

>> **MTR 0 per cent:** The investor wouldn't gain any tax benefit, meaning the cost would be the entire loss of $12,000.

Note: This list does not include the Medicare levy for the MTR ranges.

The reverse of this scenario is also true. If a property is positively geared to the tune of $12,000, the table is reversed and the tax return becomes the amount of tax paid, while the net loss becomes the net gain.

What this calculation shows is that, when an option exists, the person with the higher income should hold the negatively geared property. In a household with two incomes, you can make significant tax savings by structuring your ownership to keep in mind the tax implications of ownership.

Sole ownership can also ensure that you retain financial independence from your partner. For example, perhaps you purchased a property before you met your partner, and you turn it in to a rental property after buying a home together but retain sole ownership and complete financial responsibility for it.

Don't forget that rents rising over time eventually make almost all properties turn from negatively geared to positively geared.

Joint tenancy

Joint tenancy is a way in which two or more individuals may hold title to a property together when they own equal shares of the property. Joint tenancy is only available to individuals (not legal corporate entities), because a unique feature of holding title in a joint tenancy is the *right of survivorship*. Upon the death of one of the joint tenants, the entire ownership automatically vests in equal shares to the surviving individual or individuals without going through the probate process to ratify a will.

From a tax perspective, joint tenancy works best for two individuals, or a couple, where they're on similar tax rates and are likely to remain that way for the foreseeable future.

Joint tenancy requires unity of time, title, interest and possession, and that each joint tenant owns an equal interest or percentage of the property — so for two joint tenants, they each own 50 per cent, whereas four joint tenants would each own 25 per cent of the entire property.

Income and expenses from operating the property are reported on each individual's tax return in equal parts.

Tenants in common

A common form of co-ownership is *tenants in common* (also known as *tenancy in common*). In this ownership structure, several owners each own a stated portion or share of the entire property.

Unlike joint tenancy, in a tenants-in-common structure, owners can own a different percentage, can take title at any time and can sell their interest at any time, too. Another distinguishing characteristic is that owners have complete control over their portion of the property and can sell, bequeath or mortgage their interest as they personally decide, without any feedback from or recourse for the other owners. Further, upon their death, their share becomes part of their estate and can be willed as they see fit.

This ownership option has become more common in Australia, particularly during periods when property prices rise over an extended period. Non-couples often use tenancy in common as a way to make the purchase of property, usually as a home, affordable. Often, tenancy in common allows siblings to get together to help each other, parents to help their children into the market or friends to pool together.

WARNING

Tenancy in common is a popular way to hold title for property buyers but can be problematic unless clear understandings are in place, preferably in writing, as to who is ultimately responsible for the asset and property-management decisions (including how much money is to be spent on maintenance and when, who's in charge of ensuring bills are paid on time and, if an investment, managing the property or hiring management for it). But, even then, problems and challenges are possible:

>> **Death of an owner:** You may find that a co-owner has left her interest in a property you partially own to someone you don't get along with.

>> **Sale by an owner:** Because each owner has equal rights of control over the property, serious conflicts may arise when one owner wants to sell or borrow against the property. Or an owner may decide to sell to an individual or entity, which disrupts the spirit of cooperation among the various owners.

>> **Financial problems of an owner:** You're financially tied to your co-owners for better or worse, even in their activities other than the jointly owned property. A judgement against one of the co-owners could lead to the creditor foreclosing on that co-owner's interest in the property to satisfy a monetary judgement. Or a bankruptcy by one co-owner could lead to the court ordering a forced sale of the property to satisfy the bankruptcy creditors, unless the other co-owners are willing to pay off the creditors and buy out the financially challenged co-owner.

>> **Different plans:** Each co-owner may have a different plan for the property or the way it should be managed. With tenants in common, majority rule does not operate, and no simple way exists to arbitrate differences in opinions and goals, except through a written governing document.

CREATING AN OPPORTUNITY TO BUY

Nicola bought her first property back in 2007 with her younger brother. At the time, as a single woman earning a modest income, she didn't qualify for enough funds to purchase anything with solid investment fundamentals in Brisbane. However, by joining forces with her brother, that situation changed.

They purchased a townhouse in a middle-ring suburb of the city, and decided to own it as tenants in common — with an ownership split of 70/30 between Nicola and my brother. At the outset, they agreed on the terms going forward, which were that if either party wanted to sell their share, the other person had the first opportunity to buy that share.

Nicola and her brother lived in that property together for a number of happy years and, when her brother wanted to sell, Nicola offered to buy him out, which he accepted. A year later, she turned that property into an investment and it became the cornerstone of her portfolio — given she was able to extract equity from it twice to purchase additional investment properties over the next seven years.

Chapter **8**

Getting Your Head Around the Legal Requirements

By the time you're ready to sign on the dotted line of a contract, most of your investigative work — also known as *due diligence* — will be complete. Make sure you've done all your homework to double-check you're not making a mistake.

If you bought a residential property at auction, the time for backing out finished when you raised your paddle and your final bid was accepted. If you negotiated a private sale, you can now put conditions on the contract. But you'll sorely test the vendor's patience if you push the boundaries too far with terms and conditions.

In the previous chapter, we covered what you need to do prior to making your offer, which is essential in weeding out properties that clearly fail to meet your property goals. But you need to do many things between the time you sign the contract and the time you take control of the property. The period prior to settlement is the time to prepare for your ownership of the property, verify material facts you couldn't confirm earlier and finalise your checks of the physical condition of the purchase.

In this chapter, we track the progress of your purchase from signing the contract, through the days leading up to settlement, to the transfer of the property's title into your hands.

Offer Accepted!

For your first few property purchases, the time that you sign on the dotted line is probably one part exhilaration, one part fear. Owning a property is a huge commitment, probably the biggest financial one you've made in your life to date. When you sign the contract, you set in motion a chain of events that, in a short period (usually 30, 60 or 90 days, but it can really be any length of time agreed between the parties), will see the transfer of the property into your name or other ownership structure (with a mortgage to your bank).

At the same time that you sign the contract, you'll also usually be required to pay the agreed deposit into the selling agent's trust account. Standards for deposits differ around the country (and between estate agents), but will regularly be requested as 5 or 10 per cent of the purchase price. If you've agreed to pay $700,000 for the property, you may need to pay a deposit of $35,000 or even $70,000. However, some agents may seek a deposit of as little as $1,000. Obviously, you need to have that money available yourself or have set up a facility with a bank to do so. Don't think you can sign the contract and tell them you'll pay the deposit next week! That won't go down well.

Setting a settlement date

You've signed for the property, so when do you get your hands on it? That's generally up for negotiation between the buyer and the vendor and depends on your competing interests.

With auctions, the terms of the sale often dictate roughly when the seller wants the exchange to take place. Settlement is often advertised as 30, 60 or 90 days from the day of the auction. But, unless you've spoken to the agent before the auction and got approval for a certain period, the actual date is usually agreed at the time of signing the contract. The topic is normally addressed quite casually, such as, 'Is August 13 okay with you for settlement?'

If you're buying a residential property from an *owner-occupier* — that is, the vendor lives in the house — as is often the case, the seller may have a rigid timetable over which they have little control. The timing of the settlement probably depends on the changeover of another property that the vendor is intending to move into. Likewise, if you're purchasing the property as a home, you may have a strict date for when you need to be out of your current home (either because of settlement or an end of lease date). You may find negotiating in this position a little difficult.

TIP

For the seller, particularly if he's moving home, settlement day is likely to be more stressful than it is for homebuyer or investor. Within reason, try to be flexible. Then, when your ownership is settled, you can get move into the place or get it tenanted as soon as possible.

TIP

While trying to be flexible, you may want to flex some muscle when considering which month settlement will take place, rather than the number of days. The timing may be particularly important if you sign a contract in mid-November and settlement is negotiable — you probably won't want to take ownership in 30 days, or just before Christmas. For homebuyers, moving would be even more of a nightmare. For investors, not too many people look for places to rent around Christmas time, and students who've rented for the year often end their leases and move home. A flood of properties usually come onto the rental market at the end of November and through December. The market may not pick up again until mid- to late-January, when students (and, to a lesser extent, teachers) come back to town. This isn't to say that you'll necessarily let to students, or families with students, but students are a big influence on the market on the supply side in November and December and a big factor on the demand side in late January and February.

TIP

As for a day of the week for settlement, our preference is for a Tuesday or a Wednesday. That gives you a couple of days to have a thorough look around the property yourself after settlement. You can also organise contractors (cleaners, locksmiths, painters and so on) to do their work during those two or three days before the weekend.

Avoid Fridays for settling. If anything does go wrong with a property settlement in the middle of the week, things only get delayed by about 24 hours. But, on a Friday, 24 hours becomes Monday morning. In most real estate transactions, you won't have a problem. But when solicitors or conveyancers, or owners, can't get their act together, little can be done.

Hi ho, off to the lawyers you go

In legal terms, the transferral of property is called *conveyancing*. Depending on which state you live in, either a solicitor or a specialist conveyancing firm can do the conveyancing. And, although specialist conveyancers are not lawyers, they do perform a legal function. When it comes to property transferral, a large number of boxes need to be ticked, forms need to be filled in and government entities need to be communicated with.

When you've signed a contract, one of the first things you need to do is give the details of your solicitor or conveyancing firm to the vendor's agent. The agent usually emails the required documents to the buyer's and seller's solicitors in the next few business days and your solicitor contacts you when information is required.

WARNING

You can hire a conveyancer (either a solicitor or conveyancing specialist) at short notice, but it's best to have one in place before you either bid at auction or make an offer in a private treaty sale. Unless you're an expert on property title issues, have your conveyancing firm look over the pre-sale documentation to ensure no hidden surprises are in the contract.

WARNING

Technically, conveyancing can be performed by buyers and sellers in Australia. However, we don't recommend it. Conveyancing costs are normally between $1,000 and $2,000 and the dangers of getting it wrong far outweigh this relatively small cost. Use professionals who are experienced in the field (and make sure they have professional indemnity insurance).

Conveyancers' duties

Send the final contract to your conveyancer within a few days of signing. The conveyancer's duty is to conduct the necessary title searches (usually for set fees), coordinate the various payments to government departments and the vendor, and ensure that title has been transferred properly by the agreed settlement date.

The conveyancer's duty includes checking the current legal title owner of the property and any mortgage held, unpaid taxes and judgements, or other recorded encumbrances against the property. These searches also show any easements or third-party interests that will limit your use of the property, such as covenants and restrictions.

Removing conditions

The purchase contract can contain a number of conditions (when the property is bought through private treaty sale) that allow the buyer and seller to cancel the transaction if certain items or actions aren't satisfactory. One of three things happens with conditions: They can be approved or satisfied, unilaterally removed or waived by the beneficiary of the condition, or rejected or fail.

Conditions create a get-out clause and can be critical elements that make or break a transaction. The purchase agreement usually contains deadlines — the parties have certain rights pertaining to conditions for a limited period. For example, conditions relating to getting a satisfactory building and pest inspection may provide only ten days to make the inspection; after that, the condition is considered approved (or satisfied).

REMEMBER

The person making the condition should notify his own solicitor and the other party's agent immediately if a condition is rejected or fails. Agents aren't responsible for attempting to negotiate or mediate a resolution of any rejected condition or other deal-threatening issues that arise, but they'll often try to broker a solution.

Conducting Formal Due Diligence

With residential investment property, formal *due diligence* (checking the bona fides of the property as an investment) should really be conducted before bidding starts or the first offer is made.

REMEMBER

Performing your due diligence is the time to ask the tough questions. Don't be shy. Talk to the neighbours, the contractors or suppliers to the property, and be sure you know what you're getting. Communicate regularly and work closely with the vendor and his representatives. Value information provided in writing more highly than that provided in conversation. This period may be your best or only opportunity to seek adjustments, if important issues have been misrepresented. After the property sale is completed, it's too late to negotiate on the leaky roof.

Practical examples of due diligence include verifying the accuracy of the financial information and (for investment properties) leases presented by the seller and conducting a thorough physical inspection of the property by a licensed builder.

REMEMBER

For investors, don't underestimate the importance of reviewing the records — this review, along with the physical inspection, reveals the actual operations of the property and allows you to determine whether the property is suitable, fairly priced and meets your financial goals. The due-diligence period is your chance to decide whether you should complete the transaction or get your money back and search for a new possible acquisition. Move quickly, but thoroughly, so you don't unnecessarily hold up either yourself or the vendor in completing a sale.

Reviewing the records for larger deals

Although savvy real estate investors conduct pre-offer due diligence and often receive a copy of a pro-forma operating statements for larger property deals — such as purchasing a whole block of flats — you likely won't have an opportunity to review the actual records until you have the opportunity to conduct formal due diligence.

When you do get that opportunity, ask the vendor or property manager for all the financial data. If they are not prepared to give you everything, get what you can from them and start the process of verifying it all. The sort of information includes:

>> **Income and expense statements for the past 12 months:** The actual income and expense history should reveal any surprises that may not have been obvious from more general statements previously received from the seller. This history may show the property has a serious problem with collection of rents or unexplained out-of-control expenses that should be passed back to tenants. This examination can also give you a good idea of where to look for opportunities to improve the financial performance of the property.

>> **An accurate rent roll of tenants:** A rent roll is a list of all tenants and their important details, including move-in date, lease-expiration date, current rents, and the security deposit or bond (lodged with appropriate authorities).

- **>> A list of all tenant bonds:** When buying a new rental property, follow state laws in properly handling the tenant's security deposit. Make sure the vendor or property manager provides you detailed information on how much bond is held for each tenant and where (it should be with a state government body in cases of residential rents).

- **>> Copies of the entire tenant file of each current tenant:** Make sure you have the rental application, current and past leases or rental agreements, all legal notices, maintenance work orders and correspondence for every tenant. Also ask that the seller or property manager advise you in writing about any pending legal action involving your tenants' occupancy (and make sure your solicitor is aware of any issues).

- **>> Copies of every service agreement or contract:** Review all current contractors and service providers the current owner or property manager uses (maintenance, landscaping, pest control and so on).

- **>> A comprehensive list of all chattels included in the purchase:** The list may include appliances, equipment and supplies owned by the current property owner. *Remember:* Don't assume anything is included in the sale unless you have it in writing.

- **>> Copies of the latest utility bills:** Most tenants have to pay their own outgoings on utility usage; however, common-property utilities, if applicable to your property, will be your responsibility. Regardless, you should get as much detail on utility bills as possible, covering electricity, gas, water — including whether the property is water efficient — sewerage, garbage collection, telephone, and internet or NBN access.

REMEMBER

When you receive information, verify the accuracy of all records that you can. Most sellers are honest and don't intentionally withhold information or fail to disclose important facts; but the old adage 'buyer beware' is particularly true in the purchase of rental real estate. Questions and issues that are resolved at this time can eliminate unpleasant and contentious disagreements with your tenants in the future. The takeover of your new rental property can be chaotic, but don't fall into the trap of just verbally verifying the facts. Verify all information in writing and set up a detailed filing system for your new property. Ultimately, the best proof of the expenses is to insist on receiving copies of last year's invoices.

TIP

With experience, you'll be able to evaluate a property with surprising accuracy just by looking at the actual income and expenses, usually provided by the property manager. Look for discrepancies between the pro-forma operating statement given to you during pre-offer due diligence and the actual income and expense numbers provided.

Inspecting the property

If you've signed a private treaty sale contract, you can make the sale conditional on certain reasonable events occurring, such as suitable financing. A satisfactory building report is a must. If you haven't received a building report prior to signing the contract, make such a report a condition of your signing. The wording of 'satisfactory' shouldn't be abused, but it is vague enough so that it's up to you to be happy with the report's findings.

The real reason for making a property sale conditional on a satisfactory building report is in case you uncover unexpected nasties. All homes have faults. Older homes are more likely to have more significant faults or maintenance issues, as a factor of their age. Younger homes, however, can still have significant problems. But a building and pest-inspection report that comes back with fundamental flaws that weren't obvious to your untrained eye could provide the wriggle room to get out of the contract, or give you the ammunition to negotiate down the price initially agreed to.

TIP

If you intend to develop a portfolio of properties, getting a well-credentialed builder on your team will help.

REMEMBER

You can't put conditions on a sale when a property has been bought at auction. Building and pest-inspection reports must be done prior to auction day. Organising these reports for every property can become expensive if you continually miss out on the bidding. So, don't order these reports until the potential purchase has jumped a few other hurdles.

REMEMBER

The condition of a property directly affects its value. The prudent real estate buyer and investor always insists on a thorough physical inspection before purchasing a property, even if the property is brand new. Do a walk-through at least a few times prior to making your offer. You usually also get an opportunity to make a final inspection of your property in the week before settlement.

Your new property may look good on paper and your pre-offer due diligence may reveal no issues or concerns. But the property can be troubled by a weak link, and a physically troubled property can become a horrible place to live, and is never a good investment (unless you're planning to demolish).

TIP

You're probably making one of the biggest financial purchases and commitments of your life. Though it may feel like every cent counts when saving for a deposit, never try to save money by forgoing a proper building inspection.

Experience shows that an inspection usually pays for itself. In many cases, you're going to find items that the seller needs to correct that are greater in value or cost to repair than the nominal sum you spend on the inspection. Inspections are serious matters and not just a way to squeeze more from the seller.

The best result is if the inspection reveals no problems. Although you've spent money, knowing that your property is in good condition (at least at the time of inspection) is a great relief. That doesn't mean you won't find items in the future, possibly the very near future, that need attention.

REMEMBER

Although you can usually cancel a transaction without major penalty or loss of the deposit if your physical inspection shows the property isn't satisfactory, more often than not, an unsatisfactory report leads to additional negotiations between you and the seller. A competently prepared written inspection report provides the information you need and can serve as the basis to ask the seller to fix the problems or reduce the property's purchase price (see 'Balancing at settlement', later in this chapter).

A good building inspector has a trained eye to pick up both the obvious and not-so-obvious problems in a property. If the offer is made and accepted, the professional inspection is to identify any deal-killer problems with the property or any items that warrant renegotiation. Essentially two types of defects commonly occur:

>> **Patent defects:** Defects readily visible by simply looking at the property. Patent defects could be a broken window or a leaking tap.

» **Latent defects:** Hidden or not readily visible defects that require intrusive or even destructive testing. Examples include corroding copper pipes underneath the slab, or ceiling or window leaks that the owner has cosmetically repaired through patching and painting to hide from potential buyers.

Caveat emptor

Latin for 'Let the buyer beware', *caveat emptor* is the general rule of law for the sale of real estate in Australia. A vendor doesn't have to disclose the property's faults — it's your responsibility to know exactly what you're buying.

WARNING

Some problems won't be obvious to the naked eye. The most expensive ones usually won't stick out like the proverbial sore thumb. Electrical wiring and plumbing problems are usually hidden. Problems with the roof often won't be obvious from the ground (or inside the house). That's why buying property without having a professional spend time looking it over can be downright dangerous.

Types of inspections

Conduct your own physical inspection before making your offer. This initial overview doesn't cost anything other than your time and will keep you from wasting further time on properties that can't even pass your smell test. But it's no substitute for a professional building inspection.

TIP

Don't rush the inspection process. During the pre-offer inspection (especially for auctions), the seller must give you unfettered access to the property. If they won't make the time or they dodge making an appointment, that should serve as a warning. Don't agree to any unreasonable time or access limitations. We've seen sneaky sellers who unrealistically limit access to the property, particularly if it's occupied. Make sure that the tenants have been properly notified, as required by law and/or their lease agreements, with a liberal access period so you can thoroughly conduct all of your inspections without interference or interruptions.

Two types of professional inspections are usually performed either before offer (for auctions) or straight after the offer (for private treaty sales): Building inspections, and pest control and damage inspections.

Building inspections

Naturally, you, as the buyer, want to have all the physical aspects of the structures on your property inspected.

Areas that you want to hire people to help you inspect include

>> Doorways, walls and windows

>> Electrical systems, including all service panels and ground-fault circuit-breakers

>> Foundation, basements, sub-floor ventilation and decking

>> Heating and air conditioning

>> Illegal construction or additions and zoning violations

>> Landscaping, irrigation and drainage

>> Moisture intrusion (rising damp)

>> Overall condition of the property

>> Plumbing systems, including fixtures, supply lines, drains and heating devices

>> Roof and attic

>> Seismic, land movement or subsidence and flood risk

>> Structural integrity

WARNING

Some specific telltale signs indicate the property may have serious structural issues and require further investigation:

>> **Cracks:** Look at the entire property, including foundations, walls, ceilings, window and door frames, chimney and any retaining walls, for cracks. Don't let the seller or the agent tell you these cracks are merely settlement cracks; let your qualified property inspector or other qualified professional make that determination. A few isolated hairline cracks may be naturally occurring settlement of the structure over time, but if you can stick a screwdriver into the crack, something else may be going on.

>> **Uneven floors:** As you walk through the property, pay attention to any slant or sloping of the floors. Also watch for any soft spots in the flooring.

>> **Misaligned structure:** Your builder will look for floors, walls and ceilings that are uneven or out of plumb. A simple sign

you can check yourself is when doors or windows stick and don't open or close easily.

>> **Grounds:** Excess groundwater, poor drainage, or cracked or bulging retaining walls or concrete can be signs of soil issues such as slope failure or ground subsidence that require further inspection by an engineer. Be sure that the property drains properly and that all drains are properly installed and maintained.

>> **Moisture problems:** Look for current and historical indications of leaks such as discolouration and stains on ceilings, walls and particularly around window and door frames. Rising damp and musty odours or the smell of mould may be merely stale air or poor housekeeping; or they could indicate ongoing moisture issues. *Sump pumps* (which collect excess water and pump it away from the house) anywhere on the property are a red flag that should be explored in detail.

>> **Plumbing leaks:** Have a qualified plumbing contractor or other expert check all possible sources of leaks or moisture — under sinks, supply lines for taps, toilets, dishwashers and washing machines, plus roofs, windows, sprinklers and drainage away from the building.

Pest control and property damage

Pest-control firms are the natural choice for this type of inspection, but what they inspect is actually more than just infestations by termites and other wood-destroying insects. A thorough pest control and property damage inspection also looks at property damage caused by organisms that infect and incessantly break down and destroy wood and other building materials.

TECHNICAL STUFF

These conditions are commonly referred to as *dry rot* but, ironically they're actually caused by a fungus that requires moisture to flourish.

The report you receive from your pest control and property inspector usually includes photos of the property with notations as to the location of certain conditions noted. Some require attention immediately; others are simply areas to watch in the future.

Termites have the sort of reputation normally associated with viruses. But you usually don't need to panic if a pest-inspection report shows their existence. Ask the right questions of your inspector. Find out how much repairing any damage is likely to cost — you may get a pleasant surprise on how little the repairs cost, and it could be a great negotiating tool with the seller.

Qualifying the inspectors

Inspect the property inspectors before you hire one. As with other service professionals, interview a few inspectors before making your selection. You may find that they don't all share the same experience, qualifications and professional standards. For example, don't hire an inspector who hesitates or refuses to allow you to accompany them during the inspection.

TIP

The inspection is actually a unique opportunity for most property owners and, because you're paying, we strongly recommend that you join any inspectors while they are assessing your proposed purchase. What you learn can be invaluable and may pay dividends throughout your entire ownership. When an unscrupulous contractor later tries to tell you that you need to completely replumb your property, you can tell them to get lost if your property inspection revealed only isolated problems that you can resolve inexpensively.

Many firms can do both property and pest inspections for you, but you need to make sure of their qualifications to do one or both before you engage them. Find out what the inspectors' strengths and weaknesses are. A general builder's licence and certification as a property inspector are important, but ask if they have any specialised training in areas such as roofing, electrical systems or plumbing. These specialties can be particularly important if your proposed property has evidence of potential problems in any of these areas. For example, if a property has a history of roofing issues or mould or damp problems, an inspector who's a general contractor and a roofer is a plus.

The inspection report must be written. To avoid surprises, request a sample of one of their recent inspection reports prepared for a comparable property. This simple request may eliminate several potential inspectors but is essential to see whether an inspector is qualified and how detailed a report will be prepare for you. A simple check-the-box form may suffice for a house or apartment but, for larger properties, the more detail the better.

TIP

The advent of digital photography was a boon to property inspectors and made their sometimes mundane and difficult-to-understand reports come to life. Select a technologically adept inspector and require them to electronically send you the report, including digital photos documenting all of the conditions noted.

Although the cost of the inspection should be set and determined in advance, the price should be a secondary concern, because inspection fees often pay for themselves. Just like many other professional services, a direct correlation exists between the pricing of your inspection and the amount of time the inspector takes to conduct the inspection and prepare the report. If the inspector spends only 20 minutes at your new apartment, whatever you pay them is too much.

Using the Settlement Period Wisely

Most contracts require the seller to deliver the property in good physical condition with all basic systems in operational order, unless otherwise indicated. But the inspection process often reveals deficiencies that need to be corrected. For example, the physical and structural inspection by the property inspector may indicate the need to repair a defective electrical system.

So, with your inspection reports in hand, preferably with photographic evidence, you're prepared to contact the vendor's agent and arrange for the seller to correct the noted items at his expense. In some states, if the property is relatively new, you may be able to get the seller to have the problem fixed under builders' warranty insurance. And be aware that the seller isn't expected to fix all problems with the property, because the property is being sold as-is. The seller may be required, however, to fix any structural problems and, in most states, ensure electrical safety switches, smoke alarms and pool fences are installed and working. The seller must also attend to any breakdowns that have occurred since you agreed to buy the property (for example, a water leak has occurred, a fence has fallen over, or appliances have broken down).

TIP

If the property has problems not required to be fixed by the seller, such as cosmetic cracks in plaster or peeling paint, you may want to renovate as soon as possible, before you move in or the place is tenanted. As a buyer, use the period before settlement to your advantage and obtain all of your contractors' quotes so you're ready to begin as soon as the property settles, being wary that, until you actually own the property, you're beholden to the current owner giving you permission to get access. It may also help, if you can organise it, to have several contractors come to provide quotes at the one time, so that you're not constantly requesting access. We recommend you work out what renovations need to be done so you can get the work completed as soon as possible after settlement. If the property is an investment, you can then speak to local real estate agents about getting the property leased in advance. But be wary of signing contracts to either begin construction work or give leasing permission to an agent before taking control of the property.

Taking control at settlement

Settlement is the consummation of the real estate transaction — the goal of the buyer, seller, agents and all the other professionals who were part of the effort. It's the culmination of numerous individual acts and sometimes constant negotiation right up until the last moment. The point at which a property settles occurs only when all conditions, if any, are fulfilled, including the funding of the loan. Quite a few details must be resolved before the conveyancers (either solicitors or specialist conveyancers) can actually close the transaction.

The process or formalities of settlement are handled in different ways throughout the country. But these days the buyer and the seller usually don't need to be present. Your solicitor or conveyancer will be at the centre of activity as the essential elements come together to make your goal of purchasing anew home or an investment property a reality.

TIP

Even if your solicitor or conveyancer is handling most of the details, a few fundamental items and details still need to be addressed as you move towards settlement and before you can call the property your own. Snags are still possible, so keep an eye out for the following:

>> **Lender requests:** You or your mortgage broker need to make sure you're in contact with your lender to avoid any last-minute snags. Lenders are notorious for needing just one more signature or asking questions at the last minute about the source of your deposit or verifying your equity in

other properties. These questions aren't as random as they may seem and are usually brought up by managers who must sign off on your loan.

>> **Document errors:** Don't assume the documents are correct. Read them as thoroughly as you would any contract you need to sign.

>> **Availability of parties and busy periods:** You need to be available to review and sign the loan documents, so let the lender or your mortgage broker know if you're planning any trips around settlement time. But, during certain times of the year, things just take a lot longer. The Christmas holidays are the worst, but periods around all school holidays and long weekends can also be times when personnel plan their time off.

TIP

Most settlements occur without event, but 11th-hour issues often arise, so don't leave important details to the last minute or you may have your back to the wall, particularly if the contract contains a penalty clause to extend settlement. Documents can get lost and other unexplained communication breakdowns can occur any time when you have so many moving parts. Anticipate logistical delays and allow time for anything and everything to take twice as long as it should.

Insuring the property

Once you've signed a contract — and long before you've settled — you have an insurable interest in the property. You may not own it for three months, but if the house burns down in the meantime and the vendor doesn't have insurance, where would you be? As soon as you possibly can after signing the contract, call a reputable insurance company and organise appropriate temporary insurance, which gives you insurance for two weeks (or thereabouts) while you firm up exactly how much you need to insure the property for. Organise to pay for your insurance as soon as you can.

REMEMBER

Banks will inevitably ask whether you've insured the property prior to settlement and will probably even insist on seeing proof if you're taking a mortgage with them.

The basic insurances you want in place from day one include insuring the cost of rebuilding the home and replacing the contents. If the property is an investment, when a tenant moves in, also consider taking out insurance against tenant rental default or damage via specialist landlord insurance policies. And cover yourself with public liability insurance in case an accident occurs on your land.

EASILY TAKING POSSESSION? DON'T BET ON IT!

Nicola has been relatively lucky when it comes to issues at settlement — well, apart from the time a large branch went through a window the day before she legally owned the property (more on that soon). But one thing she always does is complete an inspection just prior to settlement to double-check everything is in order.

When Nicola made an offer on her first property with her brother (as tenants in common — refer to the previous chapter), it had an existing lease in place that was due to finish in two months. Of course, the term of the lease was legally binding unless both parties agreed for it to be terminated early. Because Nicola and her brother would be shifting into the property as their home, they had a decision to make. Should they take on the existing lease and tenants for a few months, or should they have a longer settlement? After getting expert legal advice, they decided on the latter, because it removed any potential problems with the tenancy that they may have inherited for a few months. Negotiating for settlement to be on a day after the lease had ended turned out to be a much better outcome for them.

When Nicola bought an Art Deco unit in Brisbane in 2014 after being a rentvester for a while, a huge summer storm hit the area the day before settlement. She was renting a property just down the road at the time, so was well aware of how damaging the storm had been. Very early the next morning, Nicola walked to what was going to be her new home only to find that a large branch from a tree in the courtyard had smashed through some of the ornate windows of the stairwell.

Nicola quickly called the agent and her legal representative and, within a few hours, had a formal written agreement in place that outlined how and when the damage would be repaired. Settlement was able to proceed as planned — although she did have to put up with plastic garbage bags on the windows for a few weeks.

Preparing for tenants

Although you may not be able to get into the property at will before you own it, if the property is an investment, you can start preparing it for rent-paying tenants straightaway. Draw yourself up a list of what needs to be done in the first few days of owning the property. You may find some small jobs for contractors to do; you may want to have a contract cleaner in the house or get the carpets steam-cleaned (particularly if it was owner-occupied). You may want to get started on other more significant items ASAP.

TIP

The weeks prior to settlement are also the time to interview and choose the real estate agent you'll use to manage your property. In some cases, using the agent who listed the property for sale for the vendor can be an advantage, but it always pays to assess the best property manager for the property — rather than just using the same real estate team who sold it or who have been managing it.

Balancing at settlement

When the transaction is complete and settlement has occurred, you receive a closing statement from your solicitor. Besides the actual purchase price, several expenses are incurred in the process of purchasing real estate that must be worked out. For example, the seller may have paid the council rates for the balance of the year and the buyer must reimburse the seller pro-rata.

The buyer also needs to pay expenses such as title-search fees. Table 8-1 contains some of the common expenses that are typical in the purchase of investment properties.

In addition to the allocation of expenses between the buyer and seller, the final settlement statement provided to the buyer by the solicitor or conveyancer should contain a thorough breakdown of how the final bills have been settled. The statement the buyer receives should note the final sales price (if it differs from the contract), the amount of the deposit, the starting size of the buyer's new loan, the loan fees and other fees paid in the final settling of accounts.

TIP

If the property is an investment, be sure to keep a copy of the closing statement, because this document will be used to establish your initial cost basis when you go to sell the property and need to determine your capital gain. Also, some of the expenses paid at settlement may be deductible on your tax return, such as loan fees, property taxes and insurance.

TABLE 8-1 **Typical Allocation of Expenses**

Item	Paid by Seller	Paid by Buyer
Agent's commission	X	
Mortgage discharge fee (seller's mortgage)	X	
New mortgage fee (buyer's mortgage)		X
Conveyancing	X	X
Title-transfer fee		X
Council rates		X
Stamp duty		X
Lenders' mortgage insurance		X
Loan-application fee		X
Loan-approval fee		X

Pre-settlement inspections

A vital part of every property purchase is the *pre-settlement inspection* — more commonly known as the *final inspection*. This inspection usually occurs within three days of the final settlement date, and far too many buyers don't make the most of this opportunity to walk through the property one last time.

REMEMBER

These inspections are an opportunity to double-check that the property remains in the same condition it was in on the day you signed the contract of sale, and that none of the agreed fixtures or fittings have been removed. You will only have yourself to blame if the property condition has changed during the settlement period — for example, the property has been damaged, or plumbing or electricals have failed — and you were unaware of it until after the property had become legally yours.

Your conveyancer will be able to manage this inspection for you with the selling agent.

Taking ownership

After you receive word that settlement has occurred and you're the new owner, you should get moving immediately to complete a few final checks but also so you can get your property ready to move into or leased as fast as possible if you are an investor. As soon as you can:

>> Conduct another walk-through to make sure that the property hasn't been damaged during the moving process and prior to you taking control.

>> Verify that all items indicated on the personal property inventory list are present.

>> Make sure you've received all keys (you can change locks as an added precaution, if necessary).

>> Check the utility meters. Call the utility service providers to make sure the utility company has switched the billing, so you don't get billed for the former owner's usage.

Congratulations! You're now ready to begin your property ownership journey!

Chapter **9**

Ten (Okay, Six) Signs You're About to be Stung by a Spruiker

Homebuyers and novice investors have long been blindsided by spruikers masquerading as qualified property investment professionals. And the potential financial consequences of this can be dire.

Spruikers, a bit like mushrooms, often hide in dark corners — until, in the case of the spruikers at least, property markets start to boom and buyers begin to make emotional decisions. Alas, whether they're hidden or more brazen, spruikers are generally active every day of every week, with first-time homebuyers and investors often their preferred prey.

However, a number of telltale signs can provide a strong indicator that you're about to get stung by a property spruiker. In fact, the Property Investment Professionals of Australia (PIPA) and the Property Investors Council of Australia (PICA) has outlined these six signs, and we provide some detail on each one in this chapter.

Not disclosing kickbacks or commissions

Property investment charlatans often make their money by accepting huge commissions to promote substandard property investment stock to investors. Indeed, developers commonly offer commissions of $50,000 or more — as well as luxury items such as gold Rolexes — for help with offloading subpar stock.

REMEMBER

While commissions can be a common part of the property investment sector, a qualified property investment adviser (QPIA) will disclose any commissions to their clients to ensure complete transparency in the process, and also undertake significant research before recommending a property to clients. Conversely, fake investment advisers are not QPIAs and are really only interested in making a commission from selling a property to a buyer — rather than recommending a property that is tailored to that person's specific financial plans as well as risk profile.

TIP

One of the key ways that you can differentiate a professional from a pretender is whether they are upfront and honest about any commissions they may receive from the transaction. The fake advisers and spruikers never disclose how they make their money, even if a consumer asks — and this should be a big red flag to anyone starting to become enticed by their slick marketing campaigns.

WARNING

Because these property spruikers are not QPIAs, they're under no legal obligation to reveal the commissions they receive to their potential prey.

Many professional property investment practitioners don't receive any commissions because their property investment advice is independent — these are the advisors to look out for.

Offering discounts for signing contracts immediately

Over the years, spruikers have become increasingly cunning when it comes to convincing buyers about investment 'opportunities', including enticing people more easily online.

For example, PIPA has heard of buyers being offered 'cash back' deals of tens of thousands of dollars to encourage them to buy inferior properties. Of course, the 'cash' isn't real because it's built into the sales price so, in essence, buyers are paying for their own supposed windfalls.

TIP

While negotiation is a standard part of any property purchase, an offer to 'discount' the sales price significantly as long as you sign on the dotted line immediately is a signal that everything is not as it seems.

WARNING

Not only should you have completed your due diligence (or chosen to work with qualified experts) before you submit an offer for a property, but you should also be very wary if the agent automatically offers you a big discount at your first meeting. You can bet your bottom dollar that the price reduction is no such thing at all.

Using pressure tactics

Using pressure tactics to force buyers to sign agreements, including offering discounts for immediacy, is another obvious sign you're about to do business with a spruiker.

Spruikers use these pressure tactics because they don't want you to have time to research the property yourself — let alone confer with experts on whether you are making a sound investment decision.

TIP

These types of high-pressure techniques are an attempt to get you emotionally invested in the idea that you are getting the deal of the century, when the opposite is likely to be true.

WARNING

Regardless of the type of property that you decide to buy, it is never a good idea to waive the cooling-off period (which varies depending on the state or territory in Australia where the property is located). This period is an opportunity for you to complete your research and make sure you are making a solid investment decision, and gives you the opportunity to cancel the contract within the set period.

If your state or territory doesn't have an automatic cooling-off period, consider inserting one into the contract. Of course, working with a legal professional before and during the property purchase period is vital.

Running free seminars that come with hard sells

Some of the best property investment advisers offer free educational seminars to their current and future clients. However, something these advisors would never try to do in these seminars is sell you a property!

Rather, many professional and experienced property investment advisors have a commitment to education, which is why they run seminars. Sure, they likely do so with the hope that you might engage their services, but they never run seminars that come with hard property sells.

TIP

If you're invited to a seminar — or perhaps you have seen something online and bought a ticket — don't even bother attending unless you have reviewed the bona fides of the person, or the organisation, hosting the seminar.

There is no such thing as a free lunch, so if you find yourself at a 'free' seminar that resembles cult worship and comes with a 'special offer' price for a property, then you should pick yourself up, walk out the door, and never look back!

Not following the same investment strategy

Another red flag is the spruikers not following the same investment strategy themselves — the classic 'Do as I say, not as I do' approach.

A QPIA or experienced buyers' agent will usually follow the same investment or homebuying strategy that they recommend to their clients. This strategy could be buying in blue chip locations or major regional areas, for example, or strategically selecting new homes in growth precincts.

TIP

When considering whether to work with a buying expert, either for your home or investment property, make sure you know whether they follow the same strategy that they are promoting to you. If they don't, you really must ask yourself why not.

WARNING

The domain of spruikers is to offer off-the-plan, cookie-cutter units in areas that are prone to oversupply issues. They are not interested in whether the property will make a good home or investment for you. They are trying to sell you a property, plain and simple.

Using the cut-and-run approach

Another sign you should walk (or run) away is the spruiker having a short-term mindset, such as no after-sales service.

You should understand by now that homeownership and property investment is a long-term commitment. The top property investment professionals also have this mindset when it comes to their clients. Spruikers, on the other hand, have a cut-and-run approach.

WARNING

Spruikers aren't interested in whether the property they are trying to sell you will still suit you in a decade when you might have a young family, nor do they care whether it increases in value at all. They will get paid their commission on the sale — and you will literally never hear from them again.

TIP

Experienced and professional property investment advisers will offer a tailored and bespoke approach for you personally that meets your long-term lifestyle and family requirements, or your property investment hopes and dreams.

Index

About the Authors

Nicola McDougall is an award-winning property and finance journalist, co-author of *The Female Investor: Creating Wealth, Security & Freedom Through Property* and *Property Investing For Dummies*, 3rd Australian edition, a business owner, editor, successful property investor, and the chair of the Property Investment Professionals of Australia (PIPA). *The Female Investor* won the Personal Finance and Investment category at the prestigious 2022 Australian Business Book Awards.

She is also the former editor of *Australian Property Investor* magazine and has been involved in property research, analysis and reporting since 2006.

Nicola co-founded Bricks & Mortar Media, a specialist property and finance communications and public relations firm, in 2018.

She has also been the executive manager of Corporate Affairs at the Real Estate Institute of Queensland and is considered one of Australia's most experienced and knowledgeable property journalists.

Nicola has a Bachelor of Journalism and a Master of Creative Industries (Creative Writing) from the Queensland University of Technology.

Bruce Brammall is a licensed financial adviser and mortgage broker, experienced business journalist and finance columnist, bestselling author and successful property investor. As a finance reporter and deputy business editor during his 15 years with Australia's largest selling daily newspaper, the *Herald Sun* — where he got to marry his head for numbers (somewhat rare for a journalist) with writing — Bruce covered the gamut when it came to business and economic issues. He continues to write extensively on property, superannuation, self-managed super funds, shares and the grease that oils property (mortgages and lending) for major media outlets, including News Limited's Australian newspapers (including the *Herald Sun*, the *Daily Telegraph*, *The Courier-Mail*, *The Advertiser*, the *Sunday Times* and *The Mercury*) and *The West Australian*.

In 2008, he wrote *Debt Man Walking: a 10-Step Investment and Gearing Guide for Generation X* (Wrightbooks). The book launched

Castellan Financial Consulting (now Bruce Brammall Financial, www.brucebrammallfinancial.com.au), his financial advice business, and, later, Castellan Lending (now Bruce Brammall Lending), his mortgage broking business. Prior to that he wrote *The Power of Property: Securing Your Future Through Real Estate*. They were both bestselling titles. In 2015, Bruce wrote *Mortgages Made Easy: 8 Steps to Smart Borrowing for Homes and Investment Properties*.

Bruce has a Bachelor of Arts (Communication) with a journalism major (University of Canberra), an Advanced Diploma in Financial Services (Financial Planning) and a Certificate IV in Mortgage Broking. He works in Melbourne as the principal adviser and mortgage broker with, respectively, Bruce Brammall Financial and Bruce Brammall Lending.

Bruce and Genevieve live in Melbourne with their children, Ned and Millie.

Dedication

Nicola: For my godson, Sam — you have brought me so much love and joy since the day you were born. Thank you to Julie and Noel for entrusting me to be his godmother. It is a role that I have always taken seriously and one that continues to be one of the most important and rewarding in my life. Sam, you will always be my little hero, and I can't wait to see what you achieve in your life — including property ownership since, throughout your childhood, you've been surrounded by 'property nuts' like me and your parents!

Bruce: For the troika who allowed this to happen: My wife, Genevieve, and our gorgeous tin lids, Ned and Millie. A more perfect bunch of people to hang out and spend down time with I couldn't have hoped would land in my lap. You are my reason to keep trying harder at everything. Thanks also to all of the wonderful clients and staff (Helen Savage, Ian Wood and Vikky Gallagher) of Bruce Brammall Financial and Bruce Brammall Lending. My businesses wouldn't exist if people didn't read books.

Author Acknowledgements

Nicola: My sincere thanks and gratitude go to my amazing editorial team at Wiley, especially my commissioning editor, Lucy Raymond, and publishing editor, Leigh McLennon, as well as many others at Wiley for their continued help and guidance.

I would also like to offer my sincere thanks to my business partner, Kieran Clair, for not only holding the fort in our successful small business while I devoted every spare minute to this project, but also providing valuation expertise used in this edition. Likewise, my thanks go to my Bricks & Mortar Media clients for their continued support.

Gratitude also (again) goes to my husband, Josh, and my friends and family while I secreted myself away from them all to work on this special edition.

Bruce: Ongoing thanks to those in the responsible roles at the time for making the first edition of *Property Investing For Dummies* a success, including former John Wiley & Sons general manager Lesley Beaumont, acquisitions editor Charlotte Duff and editor Kerry Davies.

Thanks to co-authors Eric and Robert for providing the original basis for the first edition of the book (published in 2008) with the US edition *Real Estate Investing For Dummies* (Wiley, 2005).

Thanks to my gorgeous wife, Genevieve, for her never-ending encouragement. And for her ongoing permission to take on these projects — they wouldn't be possible without an understanding partner. To my children, Ned and Millie, thanks for making concentration difficult. It's unusually hard to focus with you two around. And you provide the perfect reason to have a break.

Thanks to my family (Mum, Dad and Dirk), friends, Bruce Brammall Financial and Bruce Brammall Lending clients, colleagues and contacts who, over the years, have extended my property knowledge through their own investment hits and misses.

Publisher's Acknowledgements

Some of the people who helped bring this book to market include the following:

Acquisitions, Editorial and Media Development

Project Editor:
Tamilmani Varadharaj

Acquisitions Editor: Lucy Raymond

Editorial Manager: Ingrid Bond

Copy Editor: Charlotte Duff

Production

Proofreader: Susan Hobbs

Indexer: Estalita Slivoskey

Every effort has been made to trace the ownership of copyright material. Information that will enable the publisher to rectify any error or omission in subsequent editions will be welcome. In such cases, please contact the Permissions Section of John Wiley & Sons Australia, Ltd.